Dark Psychology:

Secrets of Manipulation, Mind Control, and How to Control and Influence Situations

Table of Contents

Introduction 1

Chapter 1: What Is Dark Psychology? 3

So, What About Dark Psychology? 5

What's in a Name? 8

Chapter 2: How Is Dark Psychology Used? 10

Persuasion 10

Manipulation 11

Deception 12

Hypnosis 13

Brainwashing and Other Conditioning Techniques .. 14

Gaslighting 16

General Application of Dark Psychology 17

Chapter 3: The Art of Persuasion 19

Go Ahead, Twist My Arm 19

Ancient Greek Origins of Persuasion 20

Standing the Test of Time 24

Be Stylish 26

Practicing Persuasion 27

Using Persuasion in Real Life 28

**Chapter 4: Manipulation - Where It Comes From,
How It's Used, and How to Avoid It** 31

It's Psychological 31

Using Manipulation 32

Exploiting Vulnerability 34

Why Use Manipulation? 35

Real-life Scenarios to Help You Understand Using Manipulation 36

Don't Want to Be Manipulated? 37

Chapter 5: Deception- Beyond the Little White Lie 40

Lies! 40

When Do Lies Become Deception? 42

How Lies Apply in Real Life 43

Famous Instances of Deception 45

The Art of Crafting a Good Lie 47

Pants on Fire.. 48

Chapter 6: Hypnosis- Facts, Fiction, and the Psychology That Powers It....................................50

How Mesmer Began Mesmerizing........................ 51

On to the Next Theory.. 52

The Power of Belief.. 54

Fact and Fiction in Modern Hypnosis 55

Chapter 7: The Power of Needs and Wants: Brainwashing and Stockholm Syndrome 61

The Basics Behind Brainwashing............................ 61

How Is Brainwashing Accomplished? 62

Why Does Brainwashing Work? 65

What Happens Next? 66

Coming Undone.. 67

Stockholm Syndrome 68

Lima Syndrome.. 69

Final Thoughts on Brainwashing 71

Chapter 8: Gaslighting- A History Before Hollywood 72

    The Psychology Behind Gaslighting 73

    By Any Other Name… 74

    Gaslighting, In Practice 75

    Recognizing and Avoiding Gaslighting 77

Chapter 9: Under the Radar- Recognizing Dark Psychology Before It Affects You 81

    Build Your Identity 81

    Know the Universal Red Flags 83

    Walk Away or Fight Back? 84

    Extreme Circumstances 86

Chapter 10: Come to the Dark Side- Embracing What Dark Psychology Can Do for You 88

    Why Use Dark Psychology? 88

    Is There a Lighter Side to Dark Psychology? 89

    Avoid Harming Yourself with Dark Psychology 92

Chapter 11: Dark Psychology and the Art of Seduction 95

    The Art and Science of Sex 95

    Great Seducers in History 97

    Practical and Personal Guide to Seduction 101

Chapter 12: Hostile Takeover 106

    The Internet is Telling 106

    Find Some Friends 107

    Getting the Door Open 108

    Play Nice with Others 109

    Still Nothing? 109

Break Down the Door.. 110

Abort the Mission 111

Chapter 13: Emotional Control- Manipulate or Be Manipulated 112

I LOVE YOU! 112

Put it in Reverse.. 113

Deny, Deny, Deny 114

Make Your Choice... 116

Wearing It Down 117

That's Not What I Meant!................................... 118

Chapter 14: Reading the Cues: Verbal and Non-Verbal Communications Skills to Up Your Psych Game..121

What's in a Word? 121

It Goes Without Saying 124

Applying Body Language to Dark Psychology 127

Go with Your Gut.. 129

Chapter 15: Neuro-linguistic Processing: The Art of Manipulating Yourself 130

The Origins of Neuro-linguistic Programming....... 131

The Basics of NLP 132

Taking NLP Further 135

Speaking of Journeys....................................... 139

Conclusion..140

Introduction

Welcome to Dark Psychology: *Secrets of Manipulation, Mind Control, and How to Control and Influence Situations.* By deciding to read this book, you've already made the decision to learn about the dark side of the human psyche. Within these pages, you'll find information about deception, manipulation, seduction, and much more. Learn about hypnosis, neuro-linguistic processing, and how the art of persuasion has evolved over the years.

Topics will be presented to you with historical context and modern examples, to help you better understand the discovery, development, and usage of dark psychology techniques. There are many reasons people use dark psychology and many methods behind it. Whether you want to know how to use dark psychology to your advantage or whether you are hoping to guard yourself against potential usage, this book can be your guide.

Extra care will be taken to cover concepts crucial to learning how to spot the use of dark psychology and how to counter mental and emotional attacks. This book will also open your eyes to the subtle manipulation that fills our everyday lives, from advertising gimmicks to the body language of our loved ones. Dark psychology lurks in every corner, and the only way to outsmart the people using it is to recognize it and either neutralize or reciprocate the behavior.

Within this book, you'll also find myths and methodology surrounding many of the oldest known dark psychological practices as well as new techniques based in a more high-tech society. You'll learn the difference between gaslighting and brainwashing, and find tips on spotting and guarding against these emotionally damaging methods of dark psychology. You'll also be presented with realistic scenarios to help you truly understand the power of dark psychology.

Dark Psychology: *Secrets of Manipulation, Mind Control, and How to Control and Influence Situations* is meant to be a guide and a reference to the world of dark psychology and the power of mind control. How you decide to use this knowledge is up to you, but you can be confident in knowing that you are armed with all the information you need to recognize, use, and avoid mind control as needed in any situation. The power will be in *your* hands.

We welcome you to this dark psychological study-- let's get started!

Chapter 1: What Is Dark Psychology?

To understand what dark psychology is, we first need to establish what psychology is as a whole. Psychology is defined as the study of the human mind, especially in regard to the connection between thoughts and behaviors. Even in the times of the great Greek philosophers, scholars were fascinated by the workings of the mind and how it related to our actions and reactions.

Modern psychology was founded by a German doctor named Wilhelm Wundt. Wundt was a physiologist and philosopher, and his interest in these fields led to the development of his theories about the relationship between body and mind.

In 1879, Wundt founded the world's first psychology laboratory, located at the University of Leipzig. He was determined to prove that the inner workings of the mind could be measured and examined much like any other science experiment. He developed theories and experiments based on the following principles:

- *Voluntarism*- the process of organizing the mind

- *Reductionism*- the ability to isolate each part of the mind
- *Introspection*- the ability to perform detailed self-examination

Using these principles and a modified experiment from his days in physiology, Wundt developed a method of testing the psyche of his subjects. When he was medical doctor, Wundt had tested the reaction time of his patients to certain physical stimuli in a controlled environment, like a noise or a flashing light (the precursors to modern hearing or vision tests). Wundt wondered if he could test the mind in a similar fashion.

The result was an experiment in which Wundt had his subjects concentrate on a metronome, and then describe how the metronome made them feel. By detailing the sounds, sensations, and thoughts they had when focusing on the metronome ticking, Wundt was able to begin determining the way the brain is affected by controlled stimuli. He even attempted to measure the levels of chemical activity in the brain during and after these experiments.

While Wundt's work was primitive by the standards of modern psychology, it was groundbreaking enough for him to have trained over one hundred students in the budding field, and he inspired the next generation of psychologists; Sigmund Freud, who fathered psychoanalysis; Carl Jung, who expanded upon Freud's theories and developed analytical psychology; William James, who brought modern psychology to America; and Alfred Alder, who formulated the connections between emotional needs and social skills. These men created the body of work that would blossom into the many branches of psychology and psychotherapy we see today, including cognitive-behavioral therapy.

So, What About Dark Psychology?

It can certainly be argued that dark psychology predates the study of psychology as modern science. Cleopatra is widely documented as using the art of seduction as a political negotiating tool. Didn't Adam and Eve attempt to deceive God in the first book of the Christian bible? The fact is, as long as humans have had brains, they've been using them to try and affect other people.

The term dark psychology does not refer to the opposite of psychology but is more a subset of the science of studying the behaviors of the human brain. Dark psychology can be evoked by criminologists and forensic psychologists when they are examining the behaviors of serial killers or criminal psychopaths or sociopaths. Psychopaths are those who clinically display a personality disorder which makes them particularly aberrant or aggressive towards others, and sociopaths are those who, similarly, display no emotions, conscience, or regard for societal norms or rules.

Dark psychology can also refer to the practices of deception, manipulation, or seduction for personal gain, as well as the practices of hypnosis, negative conditioning or brainwashing, or gaslighting. People use dark psychology for a number of reasons, and not all of them are negative, despite the name. Dark psychology can be used for business purposes, i.e. the use of persuasion in sales, or to help you visualize your goals, i.e. neuro-linguistic programming.

Dark psychology has been used since the dawn of early man. Deception and persuasion play into survival of the fittest. In essence, as long as humans have had thoughts in their heads, they've been thinking about how to outsmart and outwit other humans. It is only in the last century and a half that dark psychology has been studied in a modern sense, with the rise of criminology and forensic psychology as recognized sciences. Many pieces of the dark psychology puzzle were put into place well before then.

In other words, dark psychology is anything that appeals to the baser side of human thought. Dark psychology is based on instinct, gut feeling, and the ability to read others. Whether using it to fight crime, hit sales quotas, or find a lover, dark psychology is all around us. Its power lies in how we use it, how we guard ourselves against it, and how we take it upon ourselves to study it.

Over the course of the coming chapters, we're going to examine many forms of dark psychology in depth. That knowledge will be yours to keep and use as you see fit. But as we go through and discuss the history and methodology of each facet of dark psychology, take the time to ask yourself three questions, "How do I recognize this behavior in others? What could I gain from using this? What could I lose by having this used against me?"

If you can easily answer those three questions, you've probably got a strong grasp on the concept, and you'll have a much better chance of awareness when that method is being used by you or towards you. It's okay if you don't immediately know the answer to the questions. That indicates an area where you might not feel mentally or emotionally comfortable. Take time to reflect on why you're not as moved by one form of dark psychology as you are by another. Remember, even the father of psychology, Wilhelm Wundt, pushed for the principle of introspection.

What's in a Name?

If the term dark psychology sounds a bit mysterious, it's probably because it is. The brain and its functions are studied continuously in a variety of disciplines, and yet scientists, neurologists, pathologists, and those in the psychoanalytical fields consistently make new discoveries and report new findings. The human brain is a vastly complex organ, and it may yet be another few centuries before we know everything it is capable of.

One thing's for certain, dark psychology can be defined by the way people's actions and interactions affect others, for better or worse. Dark psychology is deeply rooted in cause and effect, push and pull, fool or be fooled. It relies on the ability of humans to connect with and understand other humans. It also relies on the fact that not all brains are created equal. Some people are wired to be leaders, and some are inclined to followers. Humans vary widely in intelligence, skills, and talents. Dark psychology seeks to take advantage of strengths and exploit weaknesses.

In the next chapter, we'll begin to examine how dark psychology is used by highlighting several methods, including historical and modern examples. By understanding how dark psychology can be used in almost any aspect of life, you can begin to craft your own ideas about how to use your dark psyche.

Chapter 2: How Is Dark Psychology Used?

Because dark psychology can cover such a wide variety of mental techniques, it's important to understand that each one can be applied differently. Although there is some overlap between methods, defining each one can be helpful to comprehend the full spectrum of dark psychology. Here's an overview of some of the topics this book will cover in-depth throughout later chapters.

Persuasion

To persuade someone is to convince them to act or think a certain way based on reasoning or through argument. When we talk about persuasion in the realm of dark psychology, it means to convince someone to act in a way that is beneficial to the persuader but may not be beneficial to the person being persuaded. This can come in the form of coercion or other means of forced compliance.

Persuasion is an important skill when it comes to businesses like sales, but can be used in personal relationships, as well. People who are the target of persuasion are usually aware of what is going on, but find themselves powerless to fight it. The art of persuasion as a standalone discipline has been taught since the times of the Ancient Greeks when Aristotle himself instructed his students in rhetoric and argumentative method.

Manipulation

Manipulation has a negative connotation, even before it is put under the spotlight of dark psychology. Manipulation means to bend something to your will, to mold something to your specifications and desires, or to maneuver the pieces of something until it all comes together. In dark psychology, this refers to the technique of causing another person to change themselves, act in a manner deviant from their personality, or to act on behalf of the person manipulating them.

People who are being manipulated are often unaware that it is occurring because skilled manipulators can seamlessly make their subjects feel at ease. Even if there are the proverbial red flags, they are usually quickly ignored or moved on from during the next stage of the manipulation. Psychologists are still trying to pinpoint exactly what causes a person to manipulate another, but some have identified what they believe to be the strongest characteristics of the manipulator and the manipulated.

Deception

Deception can be thought of as ranging anywhere from a small falsehood like a little white lie all the way through a large fraudulent indiscretion. Influencing how another person feels, thinks, or acts through means of untruthfulness or lies of omission all fall under the category of deception. People use deception when they've done something they do not want to have been caught doing, when they want to falsely cause someone else to think or act a certain way, or when they want to have something occur under false pretenses.

Deception can be a very hurtful method of dark psychology because most people react very negatively to being lied to. People who use deception as a method in dark psychology should be aware that there may be an aftermath of anger and grief should they be caught in their lies.

Hypnosis

Hypnosis is a technique which alters a person's state of consciousness in order to make them highly suggestible to behaviors which they would not normally exhibit. It has been used historically in everything from parlor shows to intense psychotherapy and is subject to a great deal of skepticism. In the realm of dark psychology, hypnosis could be used to cause the subject to act on another's behalf or otherwise behave in a way abhorrent to their normal state of being. Because people in a state of hypnosis are often hyper-focused on the task they've been given, they are driven to complete that task no matter the consequence.

Hypnosis was popularized by Austrian physician Franz Mesmer, whose name is where we derive the word 'mesmerize'. Mesmer's method of hypnosis is vastly different from what we think of it today, and Mesmer believed it was truly a tool for healing. Mesmer's theory held that the human body, like all things, has an invisible magnetic field and that by finding a way to align that magnetic field, his patients could be cured of what ailed them. These patients were often said to go into a trance-like state during treatment, therefore becoming 'mesmerized'.

Trance states or subconscious actions during a trance are not only limited to Mesmer's healing technique. There are numerous examples throughout history of people falling into a trance during spiritual and/or religious rituals. Many of the precursors to Mesmer's work also included magnets. It wasn't until later on, when Scottish doctor James Braid became interested in Mesmer's work, that the technique of inducing a medical trance became known as first as neuro-hypnosis and later just hypnosis.

Braid believed that mesmerism or hypnotism had less to do with magnetic fields and more to do with the process of ocular focus used to induce the trance. Braid theorized that when patients were forced to keep their eyes on a moving object, their brains were lulled into a sense of pseudo-sleep and began functioning at a different level.

Brainwashing and Other Conditioning Techniques

Most people are familiar with conditioning, made famous by Pavlov and his dogs. For those who need a refresher, Ivan Pavlov was a Russian psychologist, physiologist, and researcher who became the father of classical conditioning. His renowned experiment involving dogs can be summed up briefly like this: Pavlov would ring a bell each day, and then immediately feed his canine subjects. The dogs would begin to salivate because they knew their food was coming after the bell. Eventually, the dogs began to salivate when they heard the bell, whether they were fed immediately after or not. The dogs had become conditioned to salivate when the bell rang.

In much the same way, humans can become conditioned to behave in a specific way based on the criteria of stimuli. Brainwashing, as we often call it, can apply to an individual or a group, as is often seen in cults. People behave a certain way when prompted because they believe there will be a reward in the end. In extreme cases, people do not want to be rescued from their brainwashers, because they believe that they will be punished and not receive their promised reward.

Another extreme form of conditioning is known as Stockholm Syndrome. This occurs when a captive forms a sympathetic connection with their captor. The reverse of this is known as Lima Syndrome. Both psychological effects are named for historical acts- the first, a bank robbery in Stockholm, Sweden in which hostages refused to speak out against the bank robbers who held them against their will, and the second occurred in Lima, Peru, where militants took hundreds of people hostage at the Japanese embassy, but released most of them due to sympathy for their plight.

Gaslighting

Gaslighting is a psychological technique which existed long before it was given it modern moniker. The term 'gaslighting' comes from a play and later film called *Gaslight,* where a man makes his wife believe she is losing her sanity, when in truth, the husband is playing a series of subtle psychological tricks on her, including changing the settings of the gas lamps within their home.

In general, the term 'gaslighting' is now used to describe any number of actions which cause a subject to question their own perceptions, their grasp on reality and their sanity. Gaslighting is most frequently used by one individual on another individual, but can also be perpetrated on a larger group under certain circumstances.

General Application of Dark Psychology

As you can see, there is a multitude of techniques and methods of dark psychology, which begets some questions. Why would someone use dark psychology? How can it be used to my benefit? How do you know when dark psychology is being used on you?

The first question is the easiest to answer. People use dark psychology to get something that they want. Whether that desire is for something material or something emotional, the primary use of dark psychology is to attain a goal. That leads to another question- is dark psychology only beneficial to the person using it? Conversely, does it always harm the subject? That's a fine line, and we'll examine it in depth in later chapters, as we go over detailed techniques for the topics overviewed here.

The second question asked here was 'how can I use dark psychology to my benefit?' The answer would be to determine the method that fits your needs. To do that, you must first pinpoint your goal or desire. Once you've done that, you can determine what dark psychology method is the best way to achieve your goals. There may be times that a mixture of methods is the most effective for your needs.

As for knowing when dark psychology is being used against you, there will be a whole chapter devoted to that later on. For now, let's just say that the more you learn about dark psychology and how it works, the better prepared you will be to fend it off, which means it's time to move into our chapters detailing the techniques we've outlined. Once we've gone through the major methods, we'll talk about some other ways to recognize and use dark psychology in your everyday life, including in your love life and how to manipulate yourself to achieve your goals.

Chapter 3: The Art of Persuasion

Persuasion is one of the most ancient forms of mental manipulation, and it also applies heavily to dark psychology. Persuasion is a form of verbal manipulation which comes in the form of strong argument or debate and ends with one party changing their course of action to fit with the other party's viewpoint. We see this in everyday life in the course of business dealings and personal relationships. Persuasion doesn't always have to have a negative connotation or a dark psychological impact, but it's a useful tool to learn no matter what your desired outcome or how you choose to use the art of persuasion.

Go Ahead, Twist My Arm

The subtitle above is a phrase often used by people who are teetering towards doing something but just need a final push. Persuading them to do it is often pretty simple. But what about people who are staunch in a belief or course of action? How can you learn to use your words to have a powerful effect on others?

Think about some of the greatest 'persuaders' in human history. Who comes to mind? Political leaders and religious figures should be on your list. How about inventors and salesmen? People who are skilled in the art of persuasion are those who believe strongly enough in their convictions and have the verbal skills to impart that belief onto others.

Ancient Greek Origins of Persuasion

Persuasion has been taught as a skill and art since the days of the Greek philosophers, who instructed their students in a variety of argument and debate techniques. Aristotle was the foremost of the philosophers to teach the art of persuasion, and he presented three primary areas of focus for learning and using it.

Ethos- Ethos is a method of argument which relies heavily on the character of the speaker. Aristotle taught that in order to make a persuasive argument, the speaker must present themselves as someone who is credible and reliable. This means that in order to argue using ethos, you must choose your language carefully, and mind your appearance. Ethos arguments are well-suited (no pun intended) for business settings.

Speakers who argue using an ethos model are attempting to appear trustworthy and knowledgeable. By seemingly having more authority on a subject than their listeners, the listeners are more likely to be persuaded to come around to the speaker's viewpoint. Trustworthiness can be conveyed through verbal and non-verbal cues, through a well-groomed appearance, and the use of proper language.

This is especially true for sales and business dealings. If you want to use and ethos-modeled argument, make sure you know what the vocabulary and the uniform of that industry. People will be quick to catch on if you call a major supply item or process by the wrong name, or if you show up wearing a wildly inappropriate dress or footwear for a certain task.

Ethos arguments are meant to be authoritative and firm. When delivering one, you must be staunch in your belief, measured in your words, and relevant in your appearance. Mind your body language- it's important to be engaged with your listeners, so make eye contact and use open stances which show that you are not confrontational, just passionate. People are more likely to believe in your argument if they can sense your sincerity. You also want to make sure that you speak in a tone and timber that is strong and varying. Speaking in monotone will lose the attention of your audience.

Pathos- Arguments made on Aristotle's pathos model are arguments that are meant to play directly into the emotions of the listener. The goal of an argument or speech using the pathos model is to elicit emotion, gain the affection of your audience, and use that emotion to bring them around to your way of thinking.

In order to use a pathos-based argument, you must first understand a bit about who you are speaking to. Being able to form a rapport with the audience is key, so if you want to use a pathos model in a formal speech setting, it's important to do a little research about the people you will be interacting with. When using a pathos model argument in a personal setting, it's highly probable that you are already familiar with the emotional state of the person you are trying to persuade.

By finding a correlation between your argument and what your audience (be it one person or one hundred people) already believes, you can find a way to reach what's called their 'anchor'. Anchor points can include personal or religious beliefs, values or morals, or a set of norms specific to your audience. Finding an anchor and using it as a basis for or against your argument means you will have a solid starting point from which to base your case and appeal to their emotions.

The voice you use in a pathos model argument is also very important. Using soft, artful language is more conducive to evoking emotions such as sadness or tenderness, while strong, heavy language will strike up passion or anger. Know your purpose before you choose your words and tone, and you'll be able to craft a more effective pathos-based speech. Remember, the goal of pathos is to create a bond between you and your audience, and language will play a large part in forging that bond and bringing your listeners around to your argument.

Logos- The third style of argument taught by Aristotle is the logos model, which relies on logic and reasoning. This rhetoric can be accomplished in a number of ways, but in modern times, data and hard evidence are more readily available through internet research. This means that logos-based arguments are easier than ever to craft and to back up with sources.

Logos arguments can be extremely useful in business settings, for making sales and closing contracts. Being able to present your case, calmly and firmly with real data and logic, can take you a long way in the business world. Logos arguments are based on structure, evidence, and rhetoric, and those who wish to use this type of argument should be skilled at connecting with people through language and logic.

The goal of a logos argument is to outthink your audience. For every point and counterpoint offered, you should be able to offer another thought to contest the last. By having a strong enough argument to counter all debate, you come out with the strongest rhetoric and your audience almost has no choice but to agree with you. In short, a powerful logos argument should mean that you have the final word.

Standing the Test of Time

Aristotle's three-pronged approach to the art of persuasion has persisted for centuries because the basis of the method is never-changing but adaptable to almost any setting. Aristotle taught that all arguments need three things; a speaker, a subject, and a listener or listeners. These criteria remain the same no matter how much the world around us changes. From Aristotle's open-air schools to internet forums today, arguments are as much a part of human nature as breathing.

If you can parse your argument down to one of Aristotle's rhetorical styles while remembering the three criteria, you can successfully argue just about anything. Taking time to know your audience, research your key points, and being able to relate to others will take you a long way when it comes to the art of persuasion.

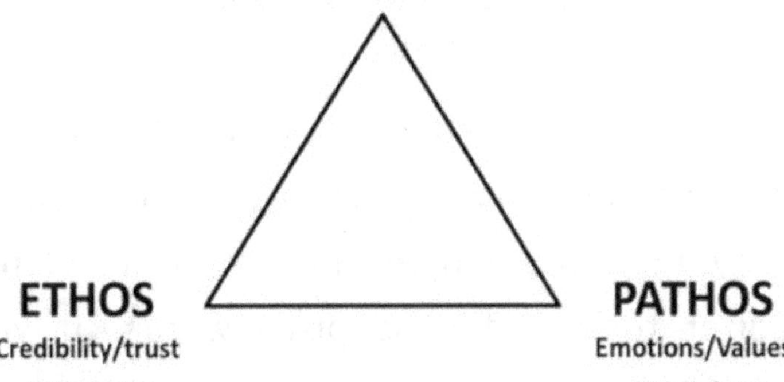

A visual breakdown of Aristotle's 3 models of arguments

Be Stylish

Aristotle also placed a heavy emphasis on the use of style when crafting a successful argument. This didn't mean he asked his students to wear their sharpest togas or finest sandals. When Aristotle talked about style, he meant language and structure that would be conducive to creating the most effective argument for the model you want to use.

For an ethos-based argument, this might mean using more formal and rigid language, to appear professional or authoritative. You want to convince your audience that you know what you're talking about, so you might want to avoid slang or loose language. In a business setting, make sure you are using proper industry terms and lingo.

When using a pathos model, choose a language which correlates with the emotion you are trying to evoke. If you are trying to be sympathetic or garner sympathy, use a softer tone and descriptive words. If you are trying to arouse anger or outrage, short, strong syllables would be more effective. Body language is important here, too. Make sure your verbal and non-verbal cues are conveying the same message.

For logos arguments, clarity is key. Aristotle taught that the facts should not be clouded by the language. Language used in a logos model should be clear, concise, and unclouded by anything that isn't a fact or doesn't have supportable evidence. Arguments in this form should be completely based in logic which cannot be easily refuted.

The way you phrase your words and how you use a tone of voice and body language is crucial no matter which model of argument you choose to use. Poor sentence structure, use of slang, sloppy syntax, and misuse of words can take the best argument and turn it on its head. Be sure to choose your words carefully and put your best mental foot forward.

Practicing Persuasion

Persuasion is a skill which for many people takes time to develop. You can study the speeches of the great persuasive orators. You can write arguments and polish them. You can have mock arguments in your head with yourself. You can practice arguing with strangers on the internet. In all seriousness, though, one of the best ways to improve your language and critical thinking skills is to read. Read things that challenge your way of thinking. Read things that make you think and create counter-arguments. Read things that are translated from other languages and pay attention to the way the words flow.

If you choose to challenge yourself, you'll be much more prepared to take on the challenge of arguing with others, and your chance of winning a persuasive argument will go up exponentially. Remember, the goal is to focus on the outcome you wish to achieve and find a verbal path to that goal.

Using Persuasion in Real Life

Learning about methods of persuasion is one thing, but using those methods in real-life scenarios is the true test of their effectiveness. Think about the ways we see persuasion used daily- let's use the example of a mother cajoling her child into doing something necessary but unwanted, like turning off their morning cartoons to get dressed and go to school. In what way could the mother use the three methods of persuasion to achieve her goal?

Using ethos, the mother could exhibit her authority over her child by telling them that if they don't want to get dressed for school, they will be grounded from the TV for a few days. The mother's willingness to flex that power over her child and her ability to follow through on the threat would persuade her child to do her bidding.

If the mother wants to use a pathos-based argument, she could sympathize with her child. Here, the mother could explain that she understands that it's rainy out and that she doesn't want to get dressed and go to work, but they both need to get started in their day before they get in respective trouble at school and work. Seeing that both mother and child are in the same situation, the child may be more willing to comply with the mother's wishes.

To use a logos argument in this situation, the mother would want to present facts to the child. She could remind them that the bus comes in 15 minutes, and she doesn't have time to drive the child today. If the child doesn't go to school, they'll have too many absences and be suspended or be excluded from a reward-based activity like a school trip or field day.

Which argument the mother decides to use would be based on the personality of her audience- her child. The mother would want to use the most effective form of argument for her child to get them to listen and comply. When using persuasion, be sure to analyze which model will best suit your purposes.

Chapter 4: Manipulation - Where It Comes From, How It's Used, and How to Avoid It

Manipulation. It's a word we hear all the time, usually in regard to personal relationships.

"He was really manipulative."

"I'm so glad I got out of that manipulative relationship."

But what does it mean? Where are the origins of manipulation in human nature? Why and how do we use it? How can we recognize and avoid when it's being used against us?

It's Psychological

When we talk about manipulation in this context, what we are really talking about is psychological manipulation. This type of manipulation is defined as having a social or psychological influence over another person or group. Social influence in and of itself is not necessarily harmful or fall under the category of dark psychology. Psychological manipulation seeks to change the perceptions or behaviors of its subject, to fulfill the desires of the manipulator.

Manipulation can also be a two-way street between the manipulator and the manipulated. People who are vulnerable to being manipulated also validate the manipulator's actions, which cycles back into a greater desire to feel that power over the manipulated.

Using Manipulation

Two basic theories have been popularized about the use of manipulation and the character of the people who use it. The first theory was developed by forensic psychologist George K. Simon. Simon believes that true manipulation is achieved through the use of covert aggressiveness. His theory holds that there are three things a manipulator must know in order to be successful:

1- How to conceal their true intentions;

2- How to determine their subject's weaknesses and vulnerabilities; and

3- How to brush aside any feelings of guilt or remorse at their actions.

According to Dr. Simon, manipulators use a large number of techniques to undermine their subjects, many of which we'll cover in-depth later in this book. Simon's list of manipulative tactics includes, but is not exclusive to:

Lies and lies of omission (deception), rationalization and minimization, denial, evasion, and diversion, shaming and vilifying, playing the victim or the servant, projection of blame, feigning innocence or confusion, and using anger as a weapon of control.

Another psychologist named Harriet Braiker centered her theory of manipulation almost entirely on the control that manipulators have over their subjects. She identified several ways in which manipulators prey on the weaknesses of their subjects in order to gain and maintain control of them. Those methods include:

1-Using positive reinforcement, such as praise, false sympathy, apologies, and gifts;

2- Using negative reinforcement, such as removing a task or request if only the subject will do what they want;

3- Using intermittent reinforcement, which causes the subject to feel unsure about whether they're doing anything correctly, or what the reward or punishment will be;

4- Causing mental trauma to convey a point, which may scar the subject and bring about anxiety about when and if the trauma will occur again; and

5- Using punishment, including verbal abuse, silent treatment, threats, blackmail, or intimidation.

Exploiting Vulnerability

Both Simon and Braiker agree that a manipulator must first find a weakness in their subject before beginning to employ manipulative tactics. Their combined inventory of emotional vulnerabilities is a veritable laundry list of the softer side of humanity. These vulnerabilities are:

1- Lack of assertiveness or the ability to stand up for themselves;

2- Being too eager to please others or being emotionally dependent on others;

3- Low self-esteem or the belief that they deserve to be treated in a manipulative manner;

4- Naivete or willingness to give their manipulator the benefit of the doubt, being a Pollyanna about the capabilities of others;

5- A lack of a strong sense of self.

Renowned psychiatrist Martin Kantor offers even more traits which make a person susceptible to becoming the subject of a manipulator. According to Kantor, not only are these people naïve, dependent, and lacking in self-esteem, they may also be narcissistic, craving the attention from the manipulator. Also, people who are vulnerable to manipulation may be materialistic, greedy, or masochistic. People who are lonely, elderly, and altruistic may also fall prey to a manipulator, as well as those who are impressionable and/or impulsive.

Why Use Manipulation?

People who use manipulation do so because they feel there is something to gain from their actions. There are several reasons why people do this, but much of it comes down to the need for power or control. There are some that use manipulation for the purpose of defrauding others, such as the many elder scams we hear about these days, and there's always the classic Nigerian prince email- send them a thousand dollars so they can send you a million! This seems too good to be true because it is. Some people use manipulation as a game, to see if they can control others, but for their own amusement, not to achieve a particular goal.

Some manipulation stems from true sociopathy, psychopathy, and other personality disorders. In these cases, especially socio- and psychopathy, the perpetrators of the manipulation are incapable of feeling empathy for others and see people as tools to be used in their game of life. They may not even be trying to hurt people, but don't know how to treat them as human beings, and therefore feel nothing when others get hurt.

Real-life Scenarios to Help You Understand Using Manipulation

Manipulation occurs every day, all around us. If we choose to be a manipulator, how can we be sure to do it effectively? Let's say you want your girlfriend to move in with you, but she's resisting because she likes the freedom of living alone. You could try a persuasion argument, but if that doesn't work, what's your next step?

You could undermine her sense of independence, but beginning to point out that one time she burned a meal and almost started a fire. Is she sure she should be living alone? You could also remind her that she needs someone to make sure she gets up for work on time because she's a heavy sleeper that sometimes misses alarms. By planting the seeds of doubt in her mind, she will begin to question her own capabilities and will come to the conclusion that she needs to live with you.

To be an effective manipulator, much like being an effective persuader, you need to know your audience. Prey on the insecurities of your subject to open their minds up to doubt. Remember, the goal of manipulation is to change your subject's perception of reality.

Don't Want to Be Manipulated?

No one wants to feel that they've fallen victim to a manipulator. It's a sinking sensation that causes self-doubt and self-loathing. It's happened to everyone-you find out a friend wasn't really a friend, you have a romantic relationship go sour, or you have an issue with a coworker that wasn't quite on the level. How can you learn to recognize the signs of manipulation before you get hurt?

There always warning signs or red flags when it comes to manipulation. Being aware of and being able to spot these signs will help you avoid the use of psychological manipulation against you. If you feel you are being manipulated, take time to look for these signs:

1- Denial of truth, especially in regard to promises made or insults hurled;

2- Use of guilt or blame, by turning everything into someone else's fault;

3- Use of anger or threats, against you or others;

4- Use of belittlement towards you for minor 'infractions';

5- Testing of limits, to see how far you can be pushed before becoming emotional;

6- Convincing you to give up something you love, like a possession or a hobby; and

7- Lying or cheating to get something they want, regardless of the cost to others.

If you can be aware enough to see these warning signs, you may be able to remove yourself from the situation or relationship before the damage is done. It's important to remind yourself that you are not deserving of manipulation and that you've done nothing to provoke it. You are not someone else's puppet or pet- be yourself and find the strength to stand up to your manipulator.

Don't be a puppet!

Chapter 5: Deception- Beyond the Little White Lie

Everyone's done it. Small children don't know who made the mess or broke the lamp. The check is in the mail. We'll be ready in five minutes. Yes, you look wonderful in that dress. The little white lie. It's inherent in human nature. Before we look at how we can use lies and deception, let's look at why we lie.

Lies!

If humans are hardwired to lie, why? Where does the instinct to tell an untruth come from? Is it biological or psychological, or both? The answer is both! Humans lie because of what scientists call a 'tend and defend' response. This means that lies are used to tend to needs or to defend against the threat, and there is a correlation between lying and the release of the brain chemical oxytocin, one of our innate 'feel good' hormones. When we have elevated levels of oxytocin, we are more likely to lie to avoid losing that feeling of a natural high.

There are several documented reasons for lying, which fall into either the tend or defend category. They are as follows:

1- Defend oneself- these are lies made to avoid punishment or backlash for action or perceived action;

2- Defend others- these are lies made to avoid others being punished or attacked for their actions or perceived actions;

3- Tend to oneself- these are lies told to gain control of a situation or a person, lies told to avoid embarrassment or awkward social situations, or lies told to gain personal desires or win admiration; and

4- Tend to others- lies told to protect others' secrets, to build other people up into greater figures than they are, and to maintain social facades.

Lies don't have to be earth-shattering, but when they become too big, it often becomes extremely difficult to keep a story straight. They say the best lies have an element of truth, and that seems to be the case. Lies often have harsh consequences when they are discovered, so if you are going to be deceptive, be sure to be emotionally prepared to deal with any fallout.

The fallout from Pinocchio's lies manifested physically as a growing nose!

When Do Lies Become Deception?

If you stop to think about lies, you'll realize that they almost have a scale. A little white lie about not having a babysitter might get you out of going to a party, so that's pretty low on the scale. But if you lie about not having a babysitter, but you don't need one because you are lying about having a baby, now that's a bit of a whopper. So where is the line?

Small lies, or fibs, often don't have many consequences. But larger lies, especially those that become compounded by repetition or addition, lead to a cycle of lying that eventually becomes destructive to self, others, or self. That cycle is most likely the definitive line between a lie and a deception.

Deception comes in many forms- lying about work or life experience, lying about the state of your relationships, lies of omission, and even lies which are told so many times, the liar themselves believe them. If lies can cause so much psychological damage, why do people still insist on using them?

How Lies Apply in Real Life

It goes back to that 'tend or defend' response. Let's take a more in-depth look at why people could use lies for those purposes. The first reason on the list was to 'defend oneself'. Self-preservation is a powerful thing. If you are in an abusive relationship, you might lie about where you've been to avoid being verbally or physically attacked, even if your location would be somewhere perfectly harmless in a healthy relationship. If your abuser thinks you were at the grocery store rather than having coffee with a friend, you've lied to protect yourself from abuse.

The second reason was to defend others. This may follow closely a scenario like above, but perhaps it's a mother lying to protect her children from a physically or emotionally abusive authority figure. Another scenario might be an older sibling taking the blame for misbehaving when it was really the younger sibling that caused a mess or broke something valuable. Friends or coworkers may lie to stick up for each other in situations that they might otherwise get in trouble for.

The next item on the list about why people lie is to tend to themselves. There are many selfish reasons to lie, and it's probably the most common reason as well. People lie to take care of their own needs and desires, in order to get what they want from others. People lie because they want other people to like them, and so they exaggerate personal accomplishments and achievements to make themselves look better. We hear of this in cases of a transcript or resume fraud.

Lies that people tell to tend to themselves also frequently are told, no maliciously, but with the intent of covering up an embarrassing situation or avoid an awkward social interaction. These lies might be to hide a slip-up or to skip a party you don't want to attend. While these are little white lies, you may still face a little backlash when your husband's annoying cousin finds out you weren't really too ill to attend her bridal shower two hours away.

The last category of lie is the one that people tell to tend to others. This can mean being deceptive about liking someone's new haircut or lying about how good someone is at their job to help them get a good reference. Lies that we tell to tend to others tend to be lies of a positive nature, but that doesn't mean that they won't be susceptible to the same negative impacts as the other types of lies.

Famous Instances of Deception

Deception is one of the most ubiquitous methods are dark psychology. We see deception used in almost every era of human history. The Trojan Horse is a fabulous example of the power of trickery and deceit. A whole population believed they were receiving a gift, and instead, ended up with a massacre.

In the modern age, one of the largest stories to come out of a basis of deception is the rise and fall of Elizabeth Holmes and her health technology business Theranos. Holmes claimed to have invented a blood testing machine which could run full diagnoses with a minute amount of blood, primarily through a finger-stick. Holmes had her investors and board of directors completely fooled, and these weren't some joes off the street.

Billionaire media mogul Rupert Murdoch, the Walton family of Walmart fame, and the DeVos family, founders of Amway, all fell prey to Holmes's deceptions as investors in her biotech firm. She even fooled many well-heeled and well-educated board members, including several former or future United States Presidential Cabinet members. Holmes's house of cards came tumbling down when it was revealed that her miraculous blood testing equipment was deeply flawed and may have even risked the health of the people who'd relied on it. Prior to her lies being discovered, Holmes had managed to accumulate a net worth of $4.5 billion, all of which is gone today.

Holmes somehow hoodwinked some of the biggest scientific and entrepreneurial names in the country and in the world. Now that's some serious deception!

The Art of Crafting a Good Lie

Telling a lie and selling a lie are two completely different things. Everyone knows when a preschooler is lying about who painted the living room wall. But when it's time to practice deception, how do you put together a story that's believable and watertight?

To tell an effective lie, it must be in part based in truth. It will be easier to remember, and you'll have a defense that you only bent the truth, not outright lied, should you get caught. You also should make your lie as simple as possible, to have fewer details to potentially mess up. If you have time to create your deception, practice telling it. It will come out much more naturally when it's time to tell it.

You shouldn't try to include anyone else in your lies-the more people who know what's happening, the greater chance of you getting caught. Lies and secrets are best kept to yourself. You should keep things brief and talk in your normal tone of voice when you deliver your lie.

Make sure your body language and eye contact match your words and be sure that you could convince yourself of what you're trying to say.

Once you've told your lie, destroy any evidence. If you made a social media post, delete it. If you wrote something down, make sure you get rid of the piece of paper. Most importantly, don't compound your lie with another lie. If you get caught, it's probably best just to confess. Why? Because if you come clean and are honest, you're less likely to get caught the next time.

Pants on Fire

Wouldn't it be wonderful if you could actually catch someone in a lie because their pants went up in flames? Unfortunately, liar, liar, pants on fire isn't a real phenomenon. There are ways to tell if someone is lying, no flames involved. Watch someone's eyes when they speak to you; if they seem unable to make eye contact or are very fidgety, they may not be being truthful with you.

Being able to spot a lie goes beyond fidgeting and shifty eyes, though. If someone has a delay in speech or a behavioral pause that they don't normally exhibit, they may be lying to you. Some experts say that a tell-tale sign of lying is if someone who doesn't normally touch their face or throat does so while speaking; likewise for playing with or running their fingers through their hair.

Speech signals could also denote when someone is lying to you. If someone repeats very simple questions before answering you, they could be buying time to craft a false response. You should also take note of any vagueness or lack of details when asked a direct question. If you suspect you're being lied to, ask the person to tell you their story again, but in reverse. The cognitive power it takes to remember a lie may make them slip up if they need to tell it out of order.

While there is no foolproof way to determine if someone is lying to you, use these tips and go with your gut, and you'll find that you'll improve your chances of ratting out a liar. Don't discount your instincts, they can tell you more than body language or speech patterns ever will.

Chapter 6: Hypnosis- Facts, Fiction, and the Psychology That Powers It

Hypnosis is, as previously stated, the subject of much skepticism, but the modern practices of hypnotherapy and the use of altered psychological states in the interrogation of prisoners would belie the number of raised eyebrows that hypnosis receives. The theory of hypnosis actually has its origins in ancient Egypt and India, where people were encouraged to heal themselves through spiritual journeys and altered states, and through 'temple sleep', a practice which encouraged people to rest in religious places to rejuvenate their minds and bodies.

In more modern times, hypnosis has taken on several different iterations, but they are all based on the theory that the mind can be controlled through a state of trance or altered state of consciousness. We're going to pick up the history of hypnosis shortly before it became popularized by Franz Mesmer.

How Mesmer Began Mesmerizing

When Franz Mesmer was a young medical student, he studied under a Jesuit monk named Father Maximillian Hell. Hell was an astronomer and researcher who was fascinated with the natural world and with the workings of the solar system, the polar regions of the earth, and the human body. Hell developed an interest in using magnets for the power of healing and introduced his student Mesmer to the technique of magnet therapy.

Mesmer took Hell's methods of magnet therapy, which basically involved using magnetized rocks to improve the flow of fluids through the body, and adapted and expanded their uses. Mesmer would often have patients swallow iron shavings, and then use a magnet to draw those shavings through the intestinal tract. Mesmer believed that people could be cured of what ailed them should he be able to get their 'vital fluid' back on track.

Mesmer called this early technique 'animal magnetism', and he truly was convinced that he could heal people through this magnetic laying on of hands. He later developed a technique which we more closely associate with hypnosis; this method involved sitting very closely with a patient while holding their hands and occasionally rubbing their shoulders, arms, and torsos while maintaining eye contact. After a while, the patients would convulse, and all their evil or poor feelings or illness would be relieved.

Skeptical yet? So were a lot of people at the time, and in 1784 a committee was formed to investigate not Mesmer himself, but one of his proteges, a doctor named d'Eslon, who had to perform Mesmer's treatments to mixed results. Why is all this important? Because the investigating committee discovered that the treatments were complete pseudoscience and that they were rooted in 'imagination'. But they worked, sometimes, so the real question is why?

On to the Next Theory

After Mesmer's works were largely downplayed and discounted, Mesmer himself retreated from medical practice, traveling Europe and living in relative obscurity until his death in 1815. A few decades later, Scottish surgeon James Braid would be the one to finally give some credence to Mesmer's practices.

Braid was a highly acclaimed physician and surgeon who pioneered a breakthrough way to treat clubfoot and other orthopedic issues of the extremities. In 1841, Braid was invited to a healing performance by one of Mesmer's former disciples, a Frenchman named Charles Lafontaine. Lafontaine allowed doctors to come onto his stage while he was using magnetic treatments and examine his patients.

Braid was among the doctors to do so, and he observed that they all seemed to be in some sort of altered mental state. While Braid had been previously completely unconvinced that magnetism was a valid medical treatment, he was so intrigued he continued to attend Lafontaine's healing demonstrations until he could formulate a working theory as to why the treatments appeared to be successful. One thing he consistently observed was that the patients all seemed to be 'awake while sleeping'.

After some consideration, Braid concluded that the patients' altered states were a result not of Lafontaine's magnets, but of his demeanor. The magnetist's behavior is what prompted the altered state, which Braid dubbed neuro-hypnosis, from the Greek for 'nervous sleep'. Braid began experimenting with the technique at home to see if he could induce the state by himself and deduced that a hypnotic state could be produced by visual or ocular fixation. This also completely debunked the use of magnets in Lafontaine's treatments.

Braid debuted his theory of hypnotism as a psycho-physiological phenomenon late in 1841, to mixed reviews from the scientific community. In his first lecture, Braid demonstrated that he could induce the same somnolent state as Lafontaine, but without the use of magnets. Although Braid had many opponents, who refused to believe that people could be healed through the power of suggestion, he would go on to integrate hypnotism into his medical practice as an alternative or complementary treatment for the relief of pain and other physical and psychological ailments.

The Power of Belief

By now, you may have come to realize that the one component of hypnosis that we haven't discussed is the patient or subject. From the early origins of medical treatments using altered states to the modern hypnotherapies we see used today, the underlying power of these methods is that the subject must *believe* that they work. The human brain is a marvelous machine, capable of higher thought and reasoning, and responsible for making sure our heart beats and our lungs breathe.

But the brain is also a biochemical mass of electrical activity and multi-layered function. While we are usually in a state of full consciousness when we are awake, our brains are constantly working on a subconscious level, which usually manifests while we sleep. Hypnosis taps into a state of mind that is somewhere in between waking and sleeping, but it does not work if the subject does not believe that it will. We've all seen performances where audience volunteers are put into a trance and asked to complete ridiculous tasks. There are movie tropes that center on a character behaving a certain way when triggered by a hypnotic keyword. How accurate are these portrayals?

Fact and Fiction in Modern Hypnosis

Let's examine some of the present-day applications of hypnosis and see what's true and what's not. Once we've done that, you'll have a clearer picture of how hypnosis plays into psychology as a whole, and how it can be applied to dark psychology, as well.

Once Braid established a baseline for modern hypnotic techniques, it became a practice which was studied by physicians and psychologists worldwide, who wanted to figure out the biology and the psychology behind the method and determine how best to use it in their practices. Hypnosis and altered states have also been studied and adopted as techniques for military usage and prisoner interrogation, including inducing trance-like states through sleep deprivation and other methods.

In contemporary medicine, hypnosis is used for pain management and anesthetic purposes in patients who may not react well to heavy pharmaceutical treatments. It is also used as an effective complementary therapy for patients with side effects from chemotherapy, those suffering from potential rejection after organ transplant, and people with autoimmune disorders such as fibromyalgia or irritable bowel syndrome.

Modern hypnotherapy is used for a wide variety of applications, the most common being to change or break a habit, or to explore thoughts that cannot be explored in a normal state of consciousness. People use hypnotherapy to quit smoking, lose weight or stop overeating, or to aid in overcoming other addictions, like gambling.

When used to access traumatic memories or examine the underlying causes of poor behaviors, hypnotherapy must be approached with great care by a skillful practitioner. Studies have shown that mishandling hypnosis in this application can lead to false memories, distortion of perception, and implantation of the therapist's own thoughts. Here is where dark psychology can come into heavy play.

A therapist with dark intentions or anyone wishing to affect someone's brain and perceptions adversely can take a subject in a state of hypnosis and wreak psychological havoc. Therapists can willingly destroy a person's psyche by planting false memories, undermining someone's sense of self and character, and creating illusions of reality which persist once someone has roused from their hypnotic state.

It's a fact, though, that not everyone can be hypnotized, and so using hypnosis as a dark psychology technique may only be effective on a certain chunk of people. But people who are highly suggestible, who are not likely to be strong-willed enough to resist, or who are already using hypnotherapy for other applications may be the perfect subjects for dark psychological uses of hypnosis.

One of the greatest examples of this is Adolf Hitler. Hitler was a young, highly insecure World War I veteran when he was treated with hypnotherapy for hysterical blindness stemming from post-traumatic stress from combat. While in an altered state, Hitler's therapist told him that only he could cure his own blindness and that he was very special and destined for great things. Hitler's therapist unwittingly conditioned him to believe that he was going to be a ruler of men and save the world from unseen evils, while in reality, he himself had become the evil.

Stage hypnotists, like we see in dinner theater, are not practicing safe hypnosis, either. Although these shows are meant to be funny, these entertainers are tapping into one of the darker sides of the hypnotic effect--the ability to induce hallucinations and psychosis. Hallucinations are the perception that something is there that is not; commonly this manifests as seeing or hearing things that are not present. Psychosis is a full-blown altered mental state, which causes people to act in a manner completely out of character for their regular behavior or personality.

A common theme of hypnosis stage shows is having people cluck like a chicken.

Hypnosis is not something to be taken lightly. It can have lasting psychological impacts on those it is practiced on. Whether those impacts are good or bad is completely dependent on the skill and the intent of the hypnotist. If you wished to learn hypnosis as a skill for implementing dark psychology, you'd have a serious weapon in your mental arsenal. It's practicality, however, is something to be considered. Because many people are not susceptible to hypnotic suggestion, its use in dark psychology has limited real-life applications.

Chapter 7: The Power of Needs and Wants: Brainwashing and Stockholm Syndrome

Brainwashing. *The Manchurian Candidate.* The Manson Family Murders. *The Bourne Identity*. The Patty Hearst kidnapping. Fictional or real-life, these are sensational cases of so-called brainwashing. Is brainwashing real and if so, how does it work? It's difficult to imagine that people can commit terrible crimes or be triggered by a keyword because they've been programmed to do so, but that's exactly what brainwashing is- reprogramming someone's brain. Updating their software, if you will.

The Basics Behind Brainwashing

Brainwashing is not a new technique, but it's a relatively new term, coined in the 1950s by a journalist named Edward Hunter. The term is from a Chinese word that translates loosely into 'wash the brain' and was used in reference to American POWs during the Korean Conflict who seemed to be overly cooperative with their Chinese captors.

Brainwashing is also referred to by a number of other names, such as thought reform, thought control, mind control, menticide, and re-education. These names give a more accurate picture of what brainwashing really is- a way to control the thoughts and actions of another person or persons through a systemic breakdown and rebuilding of their psyche.

How Is Brainwashing Accomplished?

The two major players in brainwashing are the perpetrator, known as the agent, and the subject, known as the target. Brainwashing occurs in three phases; breakdown, hope, and build-up.

During the breakdown phase, the agent begins to make an assault on the target's self-esteem and sense of identity. This can be done by telling the target that they are not who they think they are, or questioning their every move or action. Often, it will be an attack on something the target is quite proud of. Someone targeting a beautiful young woman might begin asking her why she thinks she's so attractive, or pointing out other women and exclaiming that they are much prettier than the target. The woman would begin to question her own beauty.

Another part of the breakdown phase includes the laying on of guilt. Using the scenario of the pretty girl, the agent would then make her feel guilty for the things that make her feel attractive. The agent may ask the woman why she bought some makeup or a new outfit, and if spending the money was worth it. The agent will make the target feel guilty, although there was no wrongdoing.

Once the breakdown phase has progressed to the point where the target's self-esteem and sense of self are almost completely gone, the agent will begin to attack the things the target loves- family, job, friends, etc. and ask the target to agree with them as to why those things are bad. The last part of the breakdown phase is the target losing all sense of self and wondering who they even are anymore.

It's at this point that the brainwashing enters the hope phase. The agent will begin to offer 'solutions' to the target as to how they can be saved from their terrible selves. The agent will offer some small kindnesses or suggestions of how the target can better themselves. The agent may also offer a kind ear or a shoulder to cry on, so the target can get all their negative feelings out in the open.

By giving the target hope, the agent has gained their trust. It's in this phase that the agent will also begin to reassure the target, telling them it's not their fault being the way they are, but the agent can help them fix it. The target now has something to grasp on to, but they are reliant on the agent to provide it. The target is beginning to replace their old beliefs with new beliefs but is still skeptical that the agent will provide for their needs.

If we were to continue the example of the pretty young woman through the hope phase, we would see her agent begin to tell her that despite her flaws, she could be more attractive if she tried. The agent could offer to take the target to the salon for a fresh haircut or manicure. Through these 'indulgent' actions, the agent is preparing the target for the last phase of brainwashing.

The third part of brainwashing is the buildup. Once the agent has broken down the target's self-esteem and identity and begun to 'aid' the target in regaining a sense of self, that's when the agent can drive the point home and complete the brainwashing. The agent shows the target how to act and think, in order to restore themselves and find a way to coexist with the agent in peace and harmony. Because they have been divested of their original way of thinking and acting, the target MUST comply with what the agent thinks they should do in order to be a better, more likable person.

To complete the example, in this rebuilding phase, the agent would begin to tell the target how she needs to act to finally be attractive. This is where the agent would mold the woman to his exact specification because she would desire to please him because he was so nice during the hope phase. At this point, the agent has the target convinced that his way must be the only way to be considered pretty again.

Why Does Brainwashing Work?

Brainwashing is based on psychological desires- the desire of the agent to have control of the target, and the desire of the target to please the agent. Brainwashing works because it plays to the root of the target's psyche, attacking their insecurities and offering a way to 'improve'. The agent gets the outcome they want, and the target feels that they've satisfied the agent's wishes.

The target of brainwashing doesn't necessarily have to be a 'weak-minded' person to be brainwashed. Over the course of time, plenty of strong, powerful people have fallen prey to brainwashing, including the American POWs who were the reason the word was officially coined. Those were trained military personnel who were subjected to hours, days, months, of the breakdown phase of brainwashing, and under those circumstances, anyone's inner strength could eventually give way.

That's an important takeaway and is a distinguishing factor of brainwashing, as opposed to persuasion or other dark psychological techniques. Brainwashing does not happen in a day or through the course of one persuasive argument. Brainwashing is a process that takes a great deal of time and effort on the part of the agent. The agent must themselves be mentally prepared for the commitment it takes to brainwash the target.

What Happens Next?

After the brainwashing is complete, what happens next depends on the context of the brainwashing. If the agent was a religious leader, the targets will be his followers and cult members; a good example would be David Koresh and his Branch Davidian cult. In the case of Charles Manson, he brainwashed his targets into becoming murderers for him.

In the example we used, the young woman being brainwashed into thinking she isn't attractive, chances are good that she will continue her 'relationship' with her agent. This is because she's been reprogrammed to think that she's lucky to have him because he's generous enough to think she's pretty when she follows his instructions on how to be attractive to him.

Coming Undone

Can brainwashing be reversed? The short answer is yes, but the process can be lengthy and painful. As much time as it takes to go through the brainwashing is as much time or even longer than it takes to undo the psychological damage. Targets often spend years, even the rest of their lives, in counseling to find the self that they were before the brainwashing occurred. Healing the human mind is an art and imperfect science. One of the biggest limiting factors to reversing brainwashing is that the target needs to want the reversal. Often, it takes a long time for the target to realize the extent of what's been done to them and admit that they were a victim of the agent. Only once they've realized that, can they reach out for help to begin undoing what's been done.

Stockholm Syndrome

We touched briefly on Stockholm Syndrome in the introductory chapter of this book. The term was born in 1973 after a bank robbery in Sweden, where hostages were taken and held for six days while their captor, recent parolee Jan-Eric Olsson, attempted to negotiate the release of a friend from prison. During those six days, Olsson and his four captives developed such a strong bond that when the standoff was over, the hostages refused to testify against Olsson and even defended his actions.

While no one knows exactly what happened inside that bank for those six days, one thing is clear. Olsson and his prisoners forged a bond that, under normal circumstances, would take a much longer time to create. After this incident, psychologists dissected the details and came up with four criteria that signify what came to be known as Stockholm Syndrome:

1- The hostage holds positive feelings for the captor;

2- The hostage and captor had no prior relationship;

3- The hostage refuses to prosecute, testify against, or cooperate with authorities regarding the captor; and

4- The hostage believes the captor is a good person who is acting under unusual circumstances and sympathizes with their plight.

Many years after the Stockholm bank robbery, the perpetrator, Olsson, would say that his captives made it easy not to kill them because they were well-behaved and compliant with his requests.

Lima Syndrome

In 1996, a group of guerilla militants stormed the private residence of the Japanese ambassador in Lima, Peru during a diplomatic social event attended by nearly 600 people. Although the group, the MRTA, allowed half of the party-goers to leave almost immediately, they held the other half hostage for 126 days, during which they allowed small groups of captives to leave, mostly women and foreigners. The group was protesting economical and judicial conditions in Peru and were demanding the release of some of their own from Peru's prison system, which they described as cruel and inhumane.

Over the course of what essentially became a siege, the captors began to form a bond with their remaining captives which were said to have been so unbreakable that they refused to kill a hostage for any reason. When the Peruvian armed forces stormed the home to finally end the siege, it was found that many of the MRTA members died from shots to the back of the head- they had been fleeing upstairs to protect their captives, who'd been moved for their safety from government snipers and sharpshooters.

While no MRTA guerillas survived the raid, the remaining hostages said that their captors had been courteous and kind, and had stopped threatening them with violence, instead tending to their needs and ensuring their comfort during the months-long standoff. These actions came to be dubbed Lima Syndrome, which is in essence, the opposite of Stockholm Syndrome.

Final Thoughts on Brainwashing

Brainwashing is recognized by psychological professionals and has been used as a defense in the court system, but with mixed results. The truth is, so much is still unknown about the way the human brain handles brainwashing that it is difficult to tell when someone has truly been brainwashed into committing a criminal act. If someone wished to be the agent of brainwashing, they would need to be prepared to spend a great deal of time and effort into completing the process. For those who feel they've been the target of brainwashing, they need to be prepared for the long process of reversing the damage. Although history shows us many examples of brainwashing, it rarely shows us the fallout and the recovery. As a practical method of dark psychology, brainwashing can be extremely effective, but only under the right circumstances of both agent and target.

Chapter 8: Gaslighting- A History Before Hollywood

Gaslighting is one of the most artful methods of dark psychology, and it requires a long-time commitment, similar to brainwashing. Gaslighting and brainwashing share other similarities, but gaslighting is quieter and less obvious. Like we touched upon in the overview, the term is from the title of a 1938 play by British author Patrick Hamilton.

In the play, which was later made into a film starring Ingrid Bergman and for which she won an Oscar, a young woman gives up her career as an opera singer to get married to a seemingly perfect and charming man. Once married, she begins to wonder where her husband is going during a series of absences and eventually is led to discover his terrible secret. As the story unfolds, we see her husband attempting to wear down her psyche by making her question her own sanity- this is portrayed visually by the gas lamps in their home dimming every time he is on one of his unexplained outings, which makes the woman feel as though she is losing her sense of reality.

The Psychology Behind Gaslighting

The human brain is wired to accept that what we can perceive with our senses is a reality. Things we can touch, see, hear, and smell- those things are right in front of us and therefore, they are real. When someone is being gaslit, they begin to question their perceptions and reality. Eventually, they accept that their new, altered perceptions *are* their new reality.

This is because gaslighting is, in general, very subtle. The changes happen over time, gradually, until the subject has no choice but to accept them. The brain becomes accustomed to the changes as they occur and eventually, the subject arrives at the conclusion that things must be all in their head and finally, their reality has become what the perpetrator wants it to be.

In the case of the characters in the play/movie, the perpetrator of the gaslighting is trying to hide a secret from his wife. Fearful of being found out, he crafts a plan to make his wife think that she is beginning to lose her mind, with the eventual goal of putting her in an institution and being rid of her.

The husband removes items from the home, brings new items in, and tells his wife she must have moved the items herself and claims the new items were stolen goods. Branding her a kleptomaniac, he demands she never leave the house, for her own good. Still wrought with grief over the death of her beloved aunt, the wife agrees she must be going crazy and complies with his wishes to stay home. The gaslighting is nearly complete.

Because the play and the film needed to have a happy ending, the husband's secret is revealed, and the wife is vindicated. However, that's not how things work in real life. In this day and age, we don't have gas lamps in our homes, and we don't always have happy endings. That being said, gaslighting can be perpetrated by anyone who has the time to play out a long psychological game, and subjects of gaslighting often don't see the signs until it is too late, or ever.

By Any Other Name...

Another term psychologists use for gaslighting is 'ambient abuse', and that name is pretty telling. Victims of gaslighting are subject to the psychological bidding of the perpetrator at all times. It's different from physical abuse, which occurs in a fit of violence, or verbal abuse which could be used in anger or in a more occasional form. Ambient abuse implies that even when the perpetrator and the subject are not in the same physical location, the perpetrator still has a psychological hold on their subject so that they are always 'surrounded' by the gaslighting.

Artwork of a Gas Streetlamp, by Eloise Williams

Gaslighting, In Practice

Gaslighting techniques must be subtle enough to go undetected, but strong enough to be effective. There are any number of ways to gaslight someone, including, but not exclusive to:

1- Trivializing or discrediting their feelings;

2- Withholding your true emotions, even when asked directly;

3- Countering their memories with an altered memory;

4- Refusing to listen to what they are saying;

5- Diverting their attention or questioning their validity;

6- Pretending or denying things that happened did not happen;

7- Changing the subject to avoid confrontation about your actions;

8- Show false compassion, do things for 'their own good'; and

9- Reframe behaviors, memories, and feelings to favor your desires and perspective.

Other gaslighting techniques could include changing things in your subject's life that are of importance, like erasing emails or messages and turning off alarms, to make them seem and feel irresponsible. You could move things in their home, remove or add items, and generally make them feel ill at ease wondering where those items are. The key to gaslighting is to keep it simple, take your time, and monitor your subject closely to see if you should back off or speed up the process to achieve your goals.

Recognizing and Avoiding Gaslighting

Gaslighting can happen in friendships, romantic relationships, and in work situations. By being vigilant and knowing what signs to look for, you can avoid being gaslit and feeling the sense of insecurity that comes with it.

At Work

In a work setting, gaslighting can occur when a co-worker or manager tries to sabotage your productivity or undermine the quality of your work. They may be jealous of your status, or maybe they are looking for a reason to fire you or demote you. There are several red flags to look for and ways to combat the gaslighting process. Here are some of the warning signs, and what you can do to counteract them:

1- The gaslighter says you didn't complete the work that was assigned to you, but you know it was never assigned. Be sure to keep detailed records of all the tasks you are supposed to complete and keep the emails or voice/text messages asking you to complete those tasks;

2- Objects or files keep getting moved and the gaslighter insists you moved them yourself. Take photographs of the objects or files that are going rogue, so that you know where they started and where they ended up;

3- If a suspected gaslighter tries to blame you for mistakes you know you didn't commit, be able to produce detailed documentation of your work to show your superiors; and

4- If you feel that you're being gaslighted, check and see if the perpetrator's behavior is against company policy and/or illegal.

With Friends and Partners

Close personal relationships are most often where gaslighting occurs, and the warning signs can be a little quieter than the red flags at work. If you suspect that your friend or romantic partner is gaslighting you, listen carefully to them. What they say and how they say it can be very telling. Some words and phrases to pay attention to are:

1- Why are you being so sensitive?

2- I don't think that's what happened.

3- Are you sure you're remembering that correctly?

4- I don't want to talk about it.

5- I'm not listening to your crazy talk.

6- I'm only acting this way because I love you.

7- You're always so angry.

8- You're always so sad.

9- Don't make things up.

10- Why can't you just admit that I'm right?

If you think that you're being gaslit by a friend or partner, take heart. You don't have to go along with their games. Be strong, stand your ground, and realize that you can't change the behavior of your gaslighter, but you can control how you react to it. Some manifestations of gaslighting are as follows:

1- Having a sense of unease which you cannot pinpoint;

2- Lying to avoid the anger or displeasure of your gaslighter;

3- Experiencing a feeling of losing your sanity;

4- Making excuses for your gaslighter's behavior to other people;

5- Feeling hopeless or powerless when you're with that person;

6- Wondering if your emotions are valid;

7- Having a difficult time making decisions or constantly second-guessing yourself; and

8- Questioning your self-worth or your value.

If you've been a subject of gaslighting, you should know that you can heal yourself by distancing yourself from your gaslighter and seeking professional help if necessary.

Chapter 9: Under the Radar- Recognizing Dark Psychology Before It Affects You

Dark psychology is all around us, every day. The human mind is capable of creating new and powerful ways to negatively affect other people and achieve desires by using others. It's often too late before we realize that we've been the victim of dark psychology, but if we can be vigilant and protect ourselves from the effects of dark psychology.

Build Your Identity

Find ways to be strong and confident in yourself, and you'll be less susceptible to the power of dark psychology. Self-awareness and self-esteem are crucial to protecting yourself from being mentally and emotionally violated. Take some time to think about who you are, and what you want from your life.

You should make lists for yourself- things you have accomplished, your personality strengths and weaknesses, your future goals, and how you plan to achieve them. Read the lists regularly to remind you of your self-worth. Take pride in your appearance, practicing good personal hygiene and wearing neat, clean clothes. How you look is directly tied to how you feel about yourself.

Try to eat well and get regular exercise, even if it's just a walk around the block a few times a week. Fresh air and good food go a long way towards refreshing you physically and mentally. It's also important to get quality rest. Take time for yourself, and explore new hobbies and interests. It's okay to be a little selfish sometimes- so buy some new books or art supplies, or get a fresh haircut. Small changes go a long way towards improving your outlook.

Spend time with your friends and loved ones, and avoid negative people. These are the people who will drain your energy and make you feel bad about yourself. Be kind to others and kindness will come back to you. Have a good perspective on stress. Meditate. All of these things will help you find yourself and have a better, stronger sense of self-worth.

Self-worth is often the first thing attacked by those who wish to practice dark psychology against you. If you have a strong sense of self and a strong sense of your own value, you'll be well on your way to avoiding people who might wish to harm your psyche.

Know the Universal Red Flags

Being vigilant is another good way to protect yourself from the effects of dark psychology. We've discussed some of the warning signs of the different types of dark psych in the previous chapters, but there are some universal red flags which can be used as a guideline. People who are practicing dark psychology on you will generally do the following:

1- Belittle or embarrass you purposely, often in front of others;

2- Remain emotionally distant while forcing you to be open about your emotions;

3- Downplaying or discrediting your emotions once you've shared;

4- Remind you how much you 'need' them for love, friendship, etc.;

5- Betray you by sharing personal information or stories;

6- 'Forget' things you've asked them to do or not to do;

7- Blame everyone but themselves for mistakes or misunderstandings; and

8- Not allow you to make your own decisions.

These warning signs show that the person who is trying to practice dark psychology has little regard for you, your feelings, and your well-being. Go with your gut. If you think someone is pulling any dark psychological tricks on you, remember your self-worth exercises. Step away from the relationship and avoid any further unnecessary interaction.

Walk Away or Fight Back?

It can be difficult to admit that you may have been the subject of dark psychology because no one wants to confess to being had. We all want to think that we are better and smarter than that, but in truth, anyone can fall victim to a skilled perpetrator. Remember all those business moguls that gave money to fund Theranos? The point is, you don't have to feel bad if you've been toyed with or emotionally manipulated. You can walk away. You can fight back. Here's how.

It's never easy to end a relationship, be it personal or professional. If you think that someone at work is preying on your sanity, you can find a new job, of course. That would be how to walk away. You can also fight back. Research your company's human resources policies. Find out where the disciplinary line is drawn, and then lure your coworker across it, so that you can potentially be rid of them. Chances are good that the perpetrator of dark psychology may be convinced they cannot be caught, but pride cometh before the fall, as they say. Be sure that whatever plan you form, you are always on the right side of the policy manual. No need to burn yourself lighting your coworker on fire.

If your problem is in a personal relationship, either a friendship or a romantic partnership, it's probably best to just cut things off. Shy of doing something criminal, there are only so many ways you can fight back. You want to be able to have a clean break without causing yourself undue harm in the process. It's probably easier to end a friendship rather than a romantic relationship, but even in the direst of circumstances, there's always hope.

If you live with the partner you need to break from and you feel there is nowhere to go, take heart. There are very few areas which do not have safe houses or shelters for people trying to escape abuse, be it physical or emotional. If you have a person you can trust, ask for assistance in forming a plan to get out. If you have to sneak away from your partner because a traditional breakup won't work, make sure you'll be able to access any funds you might need and that you pack your essentials. You may need to abandon the bulk of your possessions and may not be able to retrieve them, so choose wisely, or begin covertly, gradually smuggling them to a new location while you wait for the right time to make your exit.

Often, it's not possible to fight back against dark psychology in a close personal relationship. If someone is willing to use dark psych methods against you, it is highly unlikely that they will be affected by those same techniques in return. In these cases, it's better to just cut your losses, walk (or run) away, and find the help you need to begin rebuilding yourself and your life.

Extreme Circumstances

People who have highly volatile personality disorders or psychoses are often perpetrators of dark psychology, and they can be extreme in their actions and methods. Psychopaths and sociopaths are incapable of feeling empathy and will use other people with no regard for their feelings. Narcissists are out for themselves, at all costs to others as long as they are satisfied. People with a borderline personality disorder often cannot control their impulses for fulfilling personal desires.

These are obvious examples which are on the rarer side of dark psychology, but think about what people often say when they discover that someone happens to be a serial killer or serial rapist? They say how quiet they were, or that they were such a good neighbor, or, "we knew he was a little troubled, but this is just shocking!"

Ted Bundy, the subject of many studies and psychological dissection, was by all accounts a well-spoken, handsome man who was a hard worker and good friend. He was charming and personable, and he took the lives of at least 30 women. Bundy was one of those people you'd 'never suspect'. Looking at who Ted Bundy projected himself to be and who he really was, you see a picture of a perfect psychopath- one who was skilled in deception, persuasion, and manipulation.

Not all cases of dark psychology are so black and white, but by being vigilant and self-aware, you can protect yourself from becoming the subject of someone else's twisted desires.

Chapter 10: Come to the Dark Side- Embracing What Dark Psychology Can Do for You

By now, you've probably formed an opinion one way or the other about the use of dark psychology. This book is meant to show you both sides in an unbiased manner, giving you information and guidance on both utilizing and avoiding these techniques. In this chapter, we'll talk about the benefits of dark psychology, why it doesn't always have to have a negative connotation, and how to protect yourself from your own practices.

Why Use Dark Psychology?

As we've discussed, the use of dark psychology is primarily because the person using it has something they want or desire, and they are willing to affect the psyche of another person to achieve it. These desires don't always have to be something terrible or malicious, and the use of dark psychology may be a valid way to achieve that goal.

We use dark psychology when it's the path of least resistance to get what we want, and we use it when it seems that there may be no other way. Dark psychology can be used with great efficacy in business situations, like trying to close a sale or a big contract. The salesman has a desire, to sell a car, and he uses persuasion to achieve that sale. That's dark psychology in action, and you can be sure that the salesman uses his powers of persuasion every day.

Dark psychology is also used to gain control of others. This could be due to insecurity, hunger for power, or one of the psychological conditions we talked about at the end of the last chapter. Control over others can make us feel powerful and more important. Parents use dark psychology at times to control their children. Bosses use it to manage their employees. The fact is, almost everyone has used dark psychology at some point in their lives. Sometimes, we even use it unwittingly and catch ourselves later.

Is There a Lighter Side to Dark Psychology?

Dark psychology doesn't always have to be dark. Take the example of the car salesman. He's just using persuasion techniques to make a living, and it's no secret. Everyone who has ever gone to purchase a vehicle knows what type of behavior to expect from the salespeople because it takes a certain kind of personality to go into sales.

The business world is full of people who use dark psychology daily. Sometimes, the best leaders are the ones who know how to motivate their workforce using persuasion and manipulation. This doesn't have to be harmful. People can be persuaded to do good work with the promise of an equitable reward for high productivity.

Teachers use dark psychology in school to gain control of their classrooms and get their students to achieve certain goals. In the 1980s, Pizza Hut offered free pizza to children through their Book It! Program, and teachers everywhere were given a new tool in their dark psychology arsenal. Rewards are a fundamental part of any psychological conditioning.

There are entire industries based on the principles of dark psychology, not the least of which are the advertising and marketing industries. Advertising is designed to be persuasive, to point out what we are lacking and show us how a certain product will make up for that shortfall. Too fat? Diet pills will change your life! Too skinny? Get some whey powder and bulk on up! Tired? Energy drinks! The entirety of the advertising industry is aimed at persuading you to purchase things based on desires and insecurities.

Marketing is absolutely a practical application of dark psychology. With the rise of social media, it's become even more so. Marketing differs from advertising in that while advertising is all designing something that will highlight a product, marketing targets where that advertising should go for maximum effect. That's why supermarkets are laid out a particular way, or why print advertisements are placed near the feature segments in magazines. Marketing is a giant game of dark psychology, and there are people who make very good money deciding where the label should be placed on a bottle of household cleaner.

Advertising and marketing also use dark psychology when it comes to hyping trends. By playing into the human need to fit into societal norms and obtain status symbols, the advertising and marketing industry can persuade people to spend hundreds of dollars on functional items like sneakers, or convince us that we absolutely need a particular style of jeans or jacket.

The truth is, we don't need the expensive versions of those items to cover our feet or keep us warm, but by purchasing them, we've fallen victim to the dark psychology of the marketing business. They've successfully persuaded us that we are somehow less than adequate if we don't own them.

Other professions use dark psychology on a regular basis, too. Lawyers and politicians frequently use persuasion. Public speakers will often use manipulation and persuasion to get their audiences to agree with them. There are some who would argue that some religious leaders also use dark psychology to convince their congregations that they are sinners and must be guilty, terrible people.

Avoid Harming Yourself with Dark Psychology

When using dark psychology, it's important to protect yourself from yourself. It's entirely possible to employ dark psychology techniques to such an extent that you begin to become your own subject. We can do this positively, which we'll cover later when we talk about neuro-linguistic programming. However, here we're talking about the potential of negative psychological effect from using dark psychology on others.

Let's use the example of a car salesman. He needs to go to work every day and be a persuader. Through every transaction, he smiles and cajoles, singing the virtues of each car he's trying to sell. Is this his true personality? If the salesman is *always* a salesman, meaning that he's got a naturally persuasive personality, then he is probably able to navigate through life pretty easily, moving back and forth between his business and personal life with no difficult transitions.

Now let's suppose that the car salesman is not a persuader by nature. There are ways that his need to be persuasive at work can negatively affect him outside of work. Maybe having to be so 'on' at work leaves him so emotionally drained that he cannot maintain his personal relationships. Another negative effect of having to practice dark psychology in his work setting could be that dark psychology begins to creep into other parts of his personality. Maybe the salesman sees that he is capable of being persuasive at work and he begins to become persuasive outside of work, either consciously or subconsciously. If the people around him aren't fond of this change, it could also spell bad news for his personal life.

Yet another negative consequence for our salesman could be the loss of sense of self. It's possible that despite being good at persuasion during work hours, he's unhappy with the need to use dark psychology and begins to feel like a fraud. The salesman could find himself dealing with depression and low self-esteem.

The point of this example is to show how important it is to protect yourself from your own dark psychology. Don't let the use of dark psychology play on your own insecurities, and make sure to keep up your self-esteem to shield yourself from becoming your own subject. You can use all the tips that were outlined in previous chapters to craft yourself a suit of emotional armor and remember to be mentally resolved and committed to your dark psychology goal.

Chapter 11: Dark Psychology and the Art of Seduction

Ah, seduction. Even the word is a little bit sexy. Seduction is one of the world's oldest dark psychology techniques. There's a strong correlation between sex and power, and everyone knows it. Let's take a look at the psychology behind the art of seduction, some historical context to why seduction is such a powerful tool, and how you can use seduction in your own life.

The Art and Science of Sex

Sex sells. Everyone knows that. That's why people eat the terrible wings at those restaurants where the girls wear orange hot pants. Do you know the one that rhymes with 'scooters'? Scantily clad women and men adorn calendars, walk fashion runways, and are on the cover of cheeky birthday cards. Sex sells because sex appeals to our basest human desire- to procreate and extend the life of our species. That's what every living organism on this planet is programmed to do, from the smallest single-celled amoeba to every single plant, insect, and animal.

What happens to us, biologically speaking, when we are presented with the opportunity for sex? We become aroused, our heartbeats quicken, and we could become sweaty or shaky. Our hormone levels rise, and we begin to feel a kick of endorphins. Rightly so! Sex is exciting and does wondrous things to our physiology. The science of sex is a fascinating subject which researchers have been studying diligently for decades.

Sex is also an art. We see classical art students studying the human form. We see photographers making money off the trend of boudoir portraits. Burlesque is an art form which focuses solely on the anticipation of sex, not even sex itself. Why does the art of sex appeal to us just as much as science?

The answer to that is because, simply, people like to look at sexy things. We find them aesthetically pleasing. We like to think about the beauty of the human form, and we like to imagine ourselves being able to be with the beautiful people we see portrayed in magazines and performing sexy stage routines.

True seduction is a dance in and of itself, isn't it? Seduction is a two-way street because no one has ever been seduced without, albeit secretly perhaps, wanting to be seduced. Psychologists purport that seduction progresses in through five stages: identifying a potential partner or mate, establishing contact with that person, analysis of personality beyond physical attractiveness, the establishment of physical relationship, and lastly, determining whether the relationship will be continued or terminated.

The games we play to compete for the affection of others fall right under the category of dark psychology because the point of dark psychology is to find a way to get what we want. Besides sex, what more could we possibly desire, other than power? Seduction is nothing more than the perfect combination of those two things.

Great Seducers in History

Throughout human history, there are boundless stories about the power of seduction. Sex can be a weapon, it can be a way to climb a social or professional ladder, and it can be a political tool. Let's look at some of the great seducers in history and how they achieved their goals through the art of seduction.

Samson and Delilah- The Christian Bible gives us the delightful tale of the strong man with the long hair, and the woman that he thought loved him. As it turns out,

Delilah wasn't so much into Samson as she was into being an agent for the Philistines, who were mortal enemies of the Israelites, of which Samson was one.

Samson had extraordinary physical strength, which was attributed to his uncut hair. Needing to find an advantage, Delilah seduces Samson and then cuts his hair while he sleeps, robbing him of his strength and giving her Philistine tribe an edge in battle. This story of seduction and betrayal is so powerful, we still use the word 'Philistine' as a synonym for traitor.

Cleopatra- The last active pharaoh of the Ptolemaic dynasties of Egypt, Cleopatra was renowned for her beauty, her wit, her intelligence, and her political cunning. She's also famous for seducing not one, but two of the greatest Roman leaders, Julius Caesar and Marc Antony. Her relationships with these men assured protection for Egypt as well as secured trade routes and provided peace in her kingdom.

Cleopatra fell victim to her own seductions, though, when she let her emotions get the better of her and actually fell in love with Marc Antony. When they lost the naval battle of Actium to Caesar's nephew Octavian (later Caesar Augustus), it became apparent that they would not hold the leadership of Rome. Octavian invaded Alexandria, upon which Antony fell upon his own sword. Fearing she could not go on without him, the legend says that Cleopatra allowed herself to be bitten by a poisonous asp (although it was more likely a cobra), and died soon after.

Casanova- The Venetian originator of love 'em and leave 'em, Giacomo Casanova was the 18th century's 'it' boy. He lived a life of grand adventure, getting in trouble with the all-powerful Roman Catholic Church, being imprisoned for indecency, facing exile from his hometown of Venice not once, but twice, and seducing women all over Europe.

Casanova is a prime example of someone who used seduction not for power, but for fun. Casanova liked sex, he liked beautiful women, and he didn't like staying in one place for very long. Casanova was even a proponent of safe sex, reporting in his autobiography that he often used 'assurance caps'- an early rubber version of today's latex condoms. Casanova also wrote in his autobiography that everything he did was to meet his own needs for pleasure, indicating that he may have had an impulse control disorder or a sexual addiction.

Mata Hari- One of the most powerful stories of seduction in war and politics is that of Mata Hari, who was executed in 1917, accused of being a spy for Germany at the height of WWI. The Dutch-born divorcee had made a name for herself as a dancer, but as she aged, moved her act from the stage to the bedroom. Mata Hari became a courtesan, holding long-term affairs with military leaders and wealthy businessmen.

Mata Hari was tapped by French intelligence agents to use her seductiveness to sleep with the Crown Prince of Germany and bring back military secrets. However, the dancer turned courtesan turned spy allegedly let greed get the better of her and offered to sell the Germans information about the French as well. Mata Hari used her sexuality as a livelihood and a weapon of war. She was put to death by firing squad for her accused transgressions against the French.

These four examples of seduction showcase not only the various reasons we engage in seduction- personal pleasure, political clout, wartime espionage- but also the pitfalls of using sex as a tool of dark psychology.

The Altes Museum of Berlin's bust of Cleopatra, one of history's great seductresses

It's safe to say that we haven't exactly learned from history, because sex scandals are always and will always be a part of the political landscape, as well as part of our personal lives.

Practical and Personal Guide to Seduction

If you want to use seduction in your life, you'll first need to decide why you'd like to use sex to achieve your goals. To do that, you must first determine the goals. What types of goals can you set that can be reached through the use of your sexuality?

If your goal is to advance your career, there is always some truth to the old phrase "sleep your way to the top." But you don't always have to take this as far as the actual sex. Sometimes, just by being attractive and playing that card correctly, you can string along your superiors with the hint or possibility of sex. Use this to your advantage by turning the tables. While we often hear stories of people who were coerced into sex with the promise of a promotion, you *can* act in the reverse. You can use your sexuality and the art of seduction to promise sex if you receive a promotion. Whether or not you follow through is up to you.

The art of seduction at home is usually geared towards persuading a partner to do something for you or purchasing you something you really want. Sex can go a long way in the way of persuasion. Seduction can also be used for revenge or to incite jealousy. Boyfriend or girlfriend broke up with you? Seduce their best friend, or worse, someone they consider an enemy; make sure they absolutely know about.

Seduction in the political arena is well-documented through history, as we already saw in the cases of

Cleopatra and Mata Hari. They are just two of the multitudes of people who equated sex with power and put their efforts into seduction as a political tool. That being said, they both ended up dead under some pretty awful circumstances. However, most developed countries today don't have firing squads and suicide by poisonous snake seems a bit outdated. Be wary, though, of using sex to gain political power. The public backlash can be brutal and swift, especially in the social media courtroom in which we are all judged.

If you're into the art of seduction just for fun, that's a personal goal as well. Just be sure to protect yourself, practice safe sex, and try to remain emotionally detached. Everyone has their own style of seduction, but here are some guidelines and tips if you're not sure how to get started:

1- Identify the person you'd like to seduce based on the goal you've set;

2- Find out personal information about them- where they work, places they frequent, hobbies they enjoy, etc.;

3- Plot a way to get close to them, either on a date or in a group setting. Use the information you've gathered to spark conversation. You should try to look your best or do your best to be dressed appropriately for the setting or the activity.

4- Use body language to imply your interest in your subject. Make eye contact, touch their arm or shoulder when they talk, and lean close when they speak.

5- Be interested or feign interest in what they want to talk about. Let them lead the conversation. Pay attention and make a mental note of the things that seem of importance to them.

6- Take advantage of opportunities to use innuendo in the course of talking to them.

7 - If your seduction is going to play out over time, be sure to impress upon your subject how very much you are looking forward to seeing them again. Be certain they have your contact information and know that you are *very willing* to see them again soon.

8- Follow up with your subject after a day or so. You don't want to seem too eager, lest you push them away. But reaching out with a text message is a great way to keep you in their mind. Be sure to include a small detail from your conversation- like asking how a work meeting had gone or checking in to see how their ailing mother is doing.

9- Repeat steps 3 through 8 until you've achieved your goal.

This all seems very simple, but you'll have to go with your gut and realize that there are times that seduction just isn't going to play out. Perhaps once you've begun to get close to your subject, you realize they aren't the person you need to achieve your goals. Perhaps they are intuitive enough to get on to you, and they aren't interested. Remember, seduction is completed between two consenting parties- do not cross over into the criminal realm of sexual assault or worse.

You can play around with the steps above and find your own seductive style. Some people think that being true to yourself can make you feel more comfortable in your own skin during the seduction process. Others like to adopt a seduction persona. It's a matter of situational awareness and personal preference. Once the seduction is complete, it's also up to you to either maintain or terminate the relationship. This can be a difficult choice, but remember, you aren't using seduction to develop feelings, you are using seduction to achieve a goal. When the goal is accomplished, move on.

Chapter 12: Hostile Takeover

The human brain can be an open book or a locked vault. Some people are willing to share everything about themselves and their lives and some are very tight-lipped. When it comes to dark psychology, one of the biggest things you need to do is know your subject. If they don't want to talk or open up to you, how can find out what you need to know to apply dark psychology?

The Internet is Telling

We live in an era in which technology permeates every aspect of our lives. There aren't many people who don't have social media accounts, and the contents of our online spaces can tell a lot about who we are and what we love to do. Our social media shows the world what we look like, or at least the face we wish to present. We talk about our lives, our work, our homes, and our families and friends. We share our photographs and jokes and quotes that strike us as funny or inspirational.

The things we can find on social media are an amazing insight into the mind of other people. Not only can you determine someone's taste is in clothing, but you can also discover what kind of food they like, what their home looks like, and what type of people they hang out with. These are all useful pieces to the puzzle which you can use to determine if someone is a suitable subject for dark psychology.

When you're doing a little nosing around on people's social media, be sure to dig back into their older photos and posts. The person they are today isn't the person who started that Facebook account ten years ago. Look for their evolution and you'll often find their weaknesses.

Find Some Friends

If you really want to get to know someone, get to know their friends. You can learn a lot about someone by the people they surround themselves with. People are often a reflection of their family and friends. Ingratiating yourself with the people that your potential subject is close to could help you get closer to them, as well.

Talk to their friends about them; picking their brains could give you insight that looking through their social media might not be able to offer. If you can, spend time with their family. You'll be able to determine their values and maybe even get some true insider information.

If you are trying to figure out what makes your subject tick, their hobbies will also lend a big clue. Are they outdoorsy? Do they like passive or active pastimes? You can learn about what they like to do in their spare time and use that knowledge to approach them in conversation.

Getting the Door Open

If you are able to begin forming a relationship with your subject, getting them to open up to you still might not come right away. It's difficult to use dark psychology when you cannot work your way in, so here are some tips on getting someone to open up to you:

1- Set an example and be open to them first;

2- Listen well and be empathetic, even if they don't have much to say;

3- Convince them that you're a 'safe' person to talk to;

4- Don't pry, let them come to you;

5- Don't nag, that will cause them to shy away or become suspicious;

6- Take your time; and

7- Don't get frustrated. Remember that all long-term goals have a discovery phase.

Play Nice with Others

If you really want to persuade someone to open up to you, be a nice person, even if you aren't. Being able to show your subject that you're well-liked by others may convince them that you are a person worthy of friendship and trust.

Still Nothing?

Unfortunately, some people are just closed off. What can you do if you've tried all the conventional methods to get someone to open up to you, and you're still not getting a good read on them? You could just be blunt- tell them you value open communication and that you want to get to know them better. You don't have to be honest about why- use deception if you must. If you still can't get a good enough opening to begin practicing dark psychology on someone, they may be savvy about the practice themselves and are shutting you out purposely. It may be time to cut your losses and find a new subject. If you don't want to do that, it's probably time to exercise some manipulation techniques.

Break Down the Door

If you realize that you are going to have to use extreme measures to be able to practice dark psychology on your subject, it may be worth your while to step back and assess the potential psychological effects on yourself instead. Is your subject actually trying to get into *your* head? Check your warning signs, and don't become the victim.

When and if you decide to proceed with your dark psychological plan, be prepared to break down mental doors with all the subtlety of a wrecking ball. Be an overwhelming presence in the life of your subject. Bombard them with your personality. Make them think about you, and make sure they know you want to be close to them.

If you consistently insert yourself into social situations where your subject will be, they will likely begin to accept you as part of their friend group. Engage them in conversation as much as possible, using the personal knowledge you've previously gained about them. Be personable and avoid seeming as if you're stalking them, and please, don't cross into the realm of anything illegal. Just use your powers of persuasion and manipulation to become a part of your subject's life, and be sure to find ways to become a fixture in their psyche.

Abort the Mission

If you find that you have become too focused on your subject and you are beginning to feel your own mental well-being slipping, know when to step back, reassess, and walk away if necessary. You want to be the one practicing your dark psychology, not falling victim to your own desires. Some things and some people just aren't worth it.

Don't be afraid to cut your losses!

Chapter 13: Emotional Control- Manipulate or Be Manipulated

Way back in Chapter 4, we talked about the use of manipulation and how to employ and avoid manipulation techniques. Here, we'll take a more in-depth approach to handle manipulation in personal relationships, chiefly with romantic partners. There are certain ways manipulation can play heavily into these types of relationships, so let's go over what they are, how to recognize them, and how to utilize them.

I LOVE YOU!

Love-bombing. Sounds romantic, doesn't it? Love-bombing is the practice of overwhelming your brand-new boyfriend or girlfriend with affection and attention, and professing your love for them, emphatically, very early on in the relationship. Love-bombing is the psychological equivalent of a swarm of insects- you've sent so much love the way of your new partner, they cannot swat it away fast enough, and become resigned to being stung.

Love-bombing is also sometimes called love-flooding, which is another good analogy. When you employ this technique, you want to make sure you are flattering, generous with your time and with gifts, and be sure to act very sincere. The end goal of love-bombing is to make your significant other feel like no one else in the world could treat them as well as you can. When you've completed your love-bombing, they should be eating out of your hand.

Now that you know how this technique works, you also know how to recognize it if someone tries to do it to you. Be wary of anyone who seems too good to be true- they probably are!

Put it in Reverse

Reverse psychology is one of those odd areas of psychology that works in many areas but is especially effective in romantic relationships. This technique is valuable if you are with a partner who is strong-willed and tends to be contrary. It's simple. Whatever approach you would normally take in a situation, take the opposite stance.

If you are usually quick to anger, be nice to your partner. If you are normally quiet in a confrontation, be loud. Your reactions will be novel to them, and they will begin to rethink the way they see you. You can shock your partner into behaving the way you want them to. A flash of anger where there would usually be none will cause your partner to realize they've pushed a button they previously didn't know existed and will avoid the behavior that triggered your ire. If you are deceptively sweet in a situation that would normally draw anger, they will think you have softened your stance or become more understanding and will begin to show you more respect.

For you, those are the warning signs you can look for if you believe someone is using reverse psychology on you. Look for reactions that aren't what they should be, and make mental note of how often they happen. Don't fall prey to being tricked into doing things for people just because they're 'being so nice lately'.

Deny, Deny, Deny

The dark psychological practitioner giveth and the dark psychological practitioner taketh away. Love denial is the technique of giving your partner lots of love and affection when they behave in a way that is pleasing to you and taking that affection away when they misbehave. This is a form of conditioning, where your love is the reward. You can employ love denial to get your partner to comply with the way you wish them to act, dress, eat, pretty much anything.

If you want to use love denial as a dark psychological technique, it's important to lay the groundwork for it early in the relationship. Make clear to your partner that you have certain expectations of them, but don't get angry or deny love the first time they step outside the lines. Be understanding, but become harsher with each infraction. Eventually, you'll get to the point where you can fully withdraw your affections and your partner will understand that it's because they've finally gotten you to your breaking point. This is where they'll begin to comply with your desires because they don't want to push you away again.

If you suspect that love denial is being used against you, step back and examine the behaviors that you exhibited to make your partner angry. Are they that far out of line? If it seems like your partner may be overreacting to something simple or angry for some small infraction, you may be the intended victim of love denial.

Make Your Choice

Choice restriction is another dark psychology technique that works well in personal relationships. It's very simple to employ, and when used properly, is very subtle. Choice restriction is exactly what it sounds like. You give your partner a limited number of options, but just enough so that they think they still have free will.

For example, let's say you are going to go out for the evening, and your partner is rummaging in the closet for something to wear. You know they have a ton of clothing, but you want them to appear a certain way, so you suggest a particular outfit or two. It's now in their head that that's what you'd like them to wear, and psychology being what it is, they are very likely to wear what you've suggested. By the power of words alone, you've restricted their choices.

This can work on a grander scale, too, if you've been practicing your powers of persuasion. You can talk your partner into only eating specific types of foods, buying a particular style of car or clothing, and behaving in a way of which you approve. It's all about projecting the appearance of letting them have a choice, when in fact, it's your tastes and desires that are being catered to.

If you think you are having your choices restricted in your relationship, test the waters. Suggest a third restaurant option or say you don't want to wear or purchase a certain item, and gauge your partner's reaction. If they seem unduly angry that you are exercising free will or offering an option that they didn't suggest, chances are good that choice restriction is being exercised against you.

Wearing It Down

Fatigue inducement is another take on dark psychology in a relationship. In this technique, you tire your partner out until they have no choice but to comply with your wishes because it's the path of least resistance. This can be accomplished through the incessant power of suggestion, love-bombing or love-flooding, or by constantly changing the 'criteria' of your relationship. Eventually, your partner will simply give up and ask you what you want of them. It's at this stage that you can bend them to your will.

This technique requires patience on your part because it can take some time to break down your partner's emotional resistance. You can use what you learned in the brainwashing chapter to do this, or some of the manipulation or gaslighting techniques we also discussed earlier. The point of this dark psychological method is to get your partner just shy of a mental breaking point and them telling them what they can do for you to be 'saved' from their emotional distress.

Warning signs that fatigue inducement is being used on you is never being able to satisfy your partner's ever-changing demands. If you suspect that you are being deliberately worn down to be molded into compliance, make mental notes of the different ways in which your partner reacts to the same set of circumstances over a period of time. If they are consistently changing their responses, they may be trying to keep you guessing until you give up and ask what you can do to make them happy.

That's Not What I Meant!

Semantic manipulation is the practice of using words that can be interpreted in different ways to create vagaries and wiggle room which can be used as a weapon against your partner. Semantics involves crafting your words in such a way that they can have multiple meanings or interpretations. Once your partner does something according to the wishes you prescribed in your semantic phrasing, you can argue that they actually didn't comply because that's not what you actually meant. The beauty of the vagueness of semantic manipulation is that you are always right.

Because you have left things open to your partner's interpretation of your words, you can always tell them that you meant the opposite of what they interpreted. You've opened yourself up to always being correct and left them feeling defeated and second-guessing their decisions and perhaps even their own intelligence. Preying on their sense of self in this way paves the way for you to use other forms of dark psychology to gain total control.

If you think that semantic manipulation is being used against you, look for the warning signs. Does your partner always have to be right, no matter what they are talking about? Do they have volatile emotional reactions when you don't do something exactly to their liking, but they weren't specific about their desires in the first place? If your partner gives vague instructions or suggestions and then gets angry when you cannot deliver on their wishes properly, they are probably trying to employ semantic manipulation against you.

Love, they say, makes the world go 'round. If you want to make sure that your partner makes you the center of their world, utilizing dark psychology can be a powerful tool to achieve that desire.

Chapter 14: Reading the Cues: Verbal and Non-Verbal Communications Skills to Up Your Psych Game

Being able to read other people and communicate in return is a crucial skill in dark psychology. The language we use and the non-verbal signals we send and receive are an indicator of intelligence, emotional expression, and can be a portal through which to see someone's true self. People can try to mask themselves with their words, but often their body language will give them away. Let's take a crash course on verbal and non-verbal cues and skills that can help you on your dark psychological journey.

What's in a Word?

The language we use can be a telling sign of who we really are. If we are in a business setting, we want to use language that is appropriate, professional, and clear. If we are in a social setting, we may use language that contains more slang or profanity. The point is, we talk to the situation. But what if you knew that your tone of voice is actually more important than your words?

How we use our words is actually more important than *what* words we use. Think about the tone of voice you use to talk to a dog. The 'who's a good boy?' voice. No matter what you say to the dog, if you use that tone, they will wag their tail. Obviously, a dog cannot interpret your words the same way a fellow human can, but you get the idea about tone.

Framing our words in a positive way, even to communicate a negative thought, is a great way to connect to people. All psychology, dark or otherwise, relies on a basis and need to be able to form bonds that allow you access to another person's mind. By being the type of person who can speak both eloquently and situationally, you will be the type of person that others are drawn to.

You can also tell a great deal about how a person's mind works by how they speak when they are under stress. If they become flustered or speak quickly and nervously, it could be an indication that they do not handle stress well. If they speak in a voice that becomes stronger and clearer as they continue, it's a sign that their brain processes stress and adapts quickly to problems as they arise. These people are probably mentally tough and good problem solvers.

People are naturally attracted to those who can speak powerfully, because they want to be near good communicators, either because they also want to communicate or because they want to hide behind someone who can be a voice for them. Either way, you've brought them to you and now you have a modicum of power over them. You can then use your dark psychological techniques to have them help you achieve your goals.

Verbal communication skills are important and don't forget the power of the written word. People who can express themselves on paper, or via email, or a text message, have power over those that cannot because the written word is a record of our intelligence and values. We live in an era which seems to be seeing the decline of written language, due to texting abbreviations and internet acronyms.

Pay attention to how a person speaks and writes. Someone could be very intelligent and speak very intelligently, but if they write with a lot of spelling errors or texting acronyms, that could be an indicator of carelessness. Someone who takes the time to write proper sentences, even in a text message, is someone who pays great attention to detail. How we use language and the time we take to use it can tell us a lot about each other's personalities.

It Goes Without Saying

Non-verbal communication says so much without saying a word. If you truly want some insight into a person's psyche, pay attention to everything they don't say. From the way a person sits and stands to their facial expressions, being able to read non-verbal cues will make you a better and more effective communicator because you'll be able to tap into someone's emotions based on how they are carrying themselves. Let's start at the top and work our way down, as it were.

Facial expressions are probably the largest indicator of emotion for humans. They say the eyes are the window to the soul, and that's probably not too far off. People's eyes can actually have involuntary reactions to certain stimuli, like 'lighting up' when someone they love enters a room or narrowing when we feel suspicious. There probably aren't too many people who don't know what an eye roll means. Our eyes can be clouded with sadness or fatigue, and making eye contact implies sincerity or trustworthiness.

Our mouths are an indicator of feelings as well. When we smile a sincere smile, our lips open wide to reveal our teeth and gums. Fake smiles draw back the corners of our lips but do not usually reveal our teeth or gums. Frowning is the same way but in reverse. A sincere frown usually just pulls down the corners of our mouths, but a false or put-upon frown tends to be exaggerated. A grimace can indicate pain or frustration, and the latter is often accompanied by an eye roll.

Even our eyebrows can give away our emotions. A wiggle is playful, while a furrowed brow can indicate concentration or puzzlement. Raising one brow can signal skepticism, and raising both indicates surprise. Not too shabby for some vestigial patches of hair.

Once you've studied someone's facial expressions to find a clue into their feelings and emotional state, you can begin to examine the rest of their body language. People who are closed off emotionally usually display this in their posture, by keeping their arms and/or legs firmly crossed. They don't want to feel either physically or emotionally vulnerable.

People who slouch or slump often may have self-esteem issues. They want to subconsciously make themselves smaller, so no one notices them. Proud people carry themselves upright and forthright, often puffing out their chests in their own self-importance. They want to be seen. Have you ever seen a bantam rooster? They are very small in stature, but full of arrogance. They strut about the barnyard as if they are the biggest animal on the farm. People with an inflated sense of self-worth are the bantam roosters of the human world.

Someone's stance when they speak to you one-on-one is also a big indicator of how they feel about themselves and you. If they stand close to you, they are either comfortable with you or may have a cognitive disconnect about personal space. That's also useful information, as it could signal that they have cognitive dissonance in other areas of their lives. Does the person you're speaking to touch your arm or hand? They are trying to connect with you.

If someone stands a distance away, they may not feel comfortable being close to you or may be looking for a confrontation. You can use the space to your advantage because it gives you time to plan an emotional and physical escape route or plan of attack if necessary. Crossed arms or standing with hands-on-hips is a fairly obvious sign of anger, and refusing to stand directly facing you is a sign of internal conflict. The person is consciously or subconsciously trying to decide if they should continue to confront you or to turn away and leave the conversation.

When people are hurt or sad, they will often speak with their back to you, because they do not want you to be privy to their deepest emotions, or they cannot face you because you were the cause of their sadness or emotional injury. You can take advantage of this state by giving them positive attention, offering a sincere or deceptively sincere apology, and being 'the hero'. This will give you power over the person- the next time they are feeling down, they may come to you for emotional support. You've now got the ability to control their emotions when they are feeling vulnerable.

Applying Body Language to Dark Psychology

Mirroring is a bonding technique which can be used to get someone to think and feel the same things you are thinking and feeling. When you are speaking to someone, observe their posture and stance. Mimic it. When they change positions, you change positions. Do this a few times, being subtle about it of course. Once you know they haven't caught on to what you are doing, change your own stance or position. They should do the same. Continue the process until the other person consistently changes their position to mirror yours. You've now completed a subconscious bond and they should be open to your powers of persuasion or manipulation.

You can also use body language in deception. Think about the term 'poker face'. People who play cards will try to maintain as neutral an expression as possible because they do not want to signal to the other players whether or not they have a good hand. This small example of body language in deception can be used on a larger scale. People who work in the service industry often have to force a smile and a helpful attitude, even when customers are getting on their every last nerve.

If you can learn to control your own facial expressions and body language, you can successfully convince anyone that you are feeling things that you aren't really feeling. Once you can become proficient in creating false emotional projections, you can become more proficient in practicing dark psychology, because you will the tremendous tool of manipulating body language at your disposal.

Go with Your Gut

There's something to be said about gut instinct. It's a real phenomenon and can be useful in determining how someone is truly thinking and feeling. Some people just give off an air of distrust or a sense of being something that they are not. Use your intuition to read people, you may find that you are right more often than not. Sometimes we just get a bad feeling about someone- it's probably not a fluke. That's the biggest takeaway when it comes to body language; be intuitive, be observant, and be willing to be deceptive if necessary.

Chapter 15: Neuro-linguistic Processing: The Art of Manipulating Yourself

We've spent the majority of this book discussing how to read other people, how to use their emotions and actions against them using a variety of dark psychological methods, and how to protect yourself from the same happening to you. But what it the person you needed to practice dark psychology on was…yourself? That's exactly what occurs when you use neuro-linguistic programming.

Neuro-linguistic programming, or NLP, is a form of psychological manipulation that is used to set goals and program yourself to achieve them; to force you to look at your beliefs and values and change them if necessary, and to raise your self-esteem and self-confidence. Let's take a look at the history and the practice of NLP and how you can use it to become a stronger, more confident person who sets and attains goals.

The Origins of Neuro-linguistic Programming

NLP was created in the 1970s by two Americans, psychologist Richard Bandler, and linguist John Grinder. The concept was based loosely on gestalt therapy and the previous work of a counselor and psychology expert named Virginia Satir. Bandler was also a skilled computer programmer and using their combined areas of expertise, Bandler and Grinder formulated a theory that people could be programmed to perform in a certain way, just like a computer.

NLP was the culmination of a joint project by Bandler and Grinder, during which they observed the actions and thought patterns of people who were considered to be highly successful during that time. The men postulated that if they could find commonalities between those successful people and come up with a way to model those commonalities, they could help people program themselves for success.

Neuro-linguistic programming is highly based on beliefs and feelings. The originators knew that they would have to not only have to be able to offer people a very specific formula for success, but they would also have to offer the formula to people who actually believe that it works.

In more recent years, NLP has been relegated to a pseudo-science, but for the thousands and thousands of people who have been using it since its inception and in the years since, it's been a useful tool to increase self-esteem, find the power of positive thinking, set and achieve goals, and change personal beliefs and values. Let's delve into the details and you can decide for yourself if you'd like to give it a try.

The Basics of NLP

Neuro-linguistic programming is based on three principles of human excellence: strong beliefs and the willingness to examine them, good mental organization and the ability to think clearly, and awareness of the mind-body connection and how to use it.

Think of using NLP as going on a mental journey. Close your eyes and picture a door. When you open it, you are in a long corridor. This first part of the journey is where you will examine your beliefs. What do you believe in? Yourself, a higher power or religion, your friends and family? Take the time on this mental walk to really think about what you believe in and what you want to believe in.

Think of NLP as a self-guided mental journey

You can take the time during this mental walk to either decide that your beliefs are good enough for you, or determine the best way to change them in they are not. When you've walked yourself down the mental hallway and feel good about the state of your beliefs, you can imagine a second door.

On the far side of the second door is a large room, filled with shelves and objects. This room signifies your brain. How well organized is it? Do you store your thoughts and feelings in an orderly fashion, or do you let everything fall all out of sorts? By taking the time to mentally examine your own brain's filing system, you can determine whether or not you need to make conscious changes in your life.

People who are more organized, both mentally and physically, are more successful and make better leaders and businessmen. If you need to take time to get your thoughts and feelings in order, this is the part of your mental journey to do so. Once you're satisfied with how your brain is organized, you can open the door on the far side of your mental library.

On the other side of the third door is a room with two pieces of furniture. One is a magnificent throne and the other is a rough-hewn stool. Which one do you think you deserve to sit on? Try them both out. Chances are, the throne feels pretty good, but are you really good enough for it. Sitting on the stool, how do you feel? You probably feel a little downtrodden, your shoulders are slumped, and you're uncomfortable in your position. If you want to sit on the throne, you have to believe you can sit on the throne. Sit up straight. See how good that posture feels? That's how you should carry yourself- high, tall, and proud.

Savor the feeling of sitting on the throne, but don't forget the feeling of sitting in the stool. This will remind you of where you came from and where you want to be. Your mental journey is complete once you've ingrained the mental picture and feelings of sitting on the throne. You want to be able to always have that subconscious reminder to use good posture and carry yourself with pride. Congratulations! You've just completed your first baseline NLP session. How do you feel? Probably a little tired, but also pretty fulfilled.

Taking NLP Further

Once you've taken one or two maiden voyages with NLP, you can begin to use the mental journey process to set goals, make life changes, and so much more. Remember, the point of neuro-linguistic programming is right in the name:

Neuro: of the brain

Linguistic: the language we use

Programming: causing something or someone to perform a certain task

You are quite literally training your brain to think or act a particular way through the language you use with yourself. You can use the mental image of the hallway and the rooms to tell yourself you'd like to lose weight or quit smoking. Using the weight example, let's say you'd like to lose twenty pounds.

Open your first mental door as yourself, the weight and appearance you currently embody. While you walk along the corridor, think about why you'd like to lose weight and what were the factors that led to you feeling unhappy about your weight. Did you take a new, less active job where you burn fewer calories? Did you recently have an emotional upheaval that changed your eating habits? No matter the factors, you should pinpoint them and your motivation before you open the second door.

When you open that door, you'll be in a room full of food. All sorts, healthy and fatty, sweet and salty, fresh and processed. There will be all sorts of people in this room, too- thin, fat, tall, short, healthy and sallow. Look at the food choices those people are making and how they appear to you. Which of the people in this room do you want to model your eating habits? When you've observed everything that's happening in that room and come to a conclusion about how you want to look and how you should eat, open the third door.

In the last room, imagine yourself as you want to be and look. Take a good mental picture. Now think of something absurd that you could do with the unhealthy foods you're resolving to avoid. Picture a cliff you could throw fried foods off of, into a deep abyss. Picture putting bags of chips in a catapult and launching them out of your life. Yes, this sounds ridiculous, but you're trying to make a mental impression on yourself. When you are done mentally ridding yourself of junk food, open your eyes and go about your business. But whenever temptation strikes, think about your chip catapult. You'll give yourself a good chuckle, and avoid eating the chips.

Another way you could handle the last room is by convincing yourself that the food you want to eat tastes terrible. Imagine yourself eating a fast-food hamburger, but imagine that burger is bitter and unpalatable. The next time you think about fast food, you'll have left yourself with the impression that it doesn't even taste very good.

Other applications of NLP could be to form better study habits, to examine your personal beliefs on a more detailed level, to teach yourself to have better self-esteem, or to resolve emotional issues. Once learned, NLP is one of the most useful tools you can use to manipulate yourself and when you've learned the art of manipulating yourself, you'll be that much stronger to defend yourself from manipulation by other people. You'll also have a better grasp on manipulating others and practicing other forms of dark psychology.

NLP can take a little time to become adept at, but it's such a versatile method of introspection and self-manipulation, the time put in to learn it is well worth it. If you try it and fail a few times, don't give up. The more you practice NLP, the easier it will become. Try to practice your NLP in a quiet place where you aren't likely to be interrupted. Play a little background music for yourself if you like, or any other kind of ambient noise which will help you relax. One of the keys to practicing good NLP is to allow your mind to both wander and be hyper-focused, and if you're feeling uncomfortable or stressed, chances are good that your NLP session won't be nearly as effective.

Eventually, you'll become so skilled at NLP that even when you need to give yourself a little pep talk, you can close your eyes and sprint through your mental corridors to give yourself a quick refresher or mental pick-me-up. You can also do this to quickly reaffirm or reassess a thought or belief. NLP is a practice that you can put to use any time you need to work through a problem or a tough situation. You may even become so skilled that you can teach others or take them on a guided mental journey towards their goals. Or yours- remember, the mental power is in your hands.

Speaking of Journeys...

With this discussion on neuro-linguistic programming and teaching your brain to take a mental journey, our journey together through the world of dark psychology has come to a close. The information you've received in this book should serve as a guide to you on your path to discovering how dark psych can work for you and against you and how to handle dark psychology when it presents itself to you. Remember to always go with your gut, if all else fails, and be an observer and active participant in the world around you. It's only through knowing and interacting with humanity, can we truly learn how to control it.

Conclusion

Thank you for taking the time to go through this study of dark psychology. This book covered a lot of topics and if you felt overwhelmed by any of it, please think of these chapters as a reference, which you can read and study over and over.

It was important to include ways to both use and avoid dark psychology because you should make your own decisions about its applications and how you'd like to employ them. It should be stressed that at no time, should anyone use the advice in this book to commit any acts that are or could be illegal.

Dark Psychology: *Secrets of Manipulation, Mind Control, and How to Control and Influence Situations* should be used as a textbook, a reference, and a guide to dark psychology. We covered the most prominent techniques, their histories, their practices in today's modern society, and how to recognize the signs of other people using dark psychology.

One thing about human nature is, the more things change, the more they stay the same. Yes, modern stressors and stimuli may be different from those in eras past, but humans themselves will always react with emotion and be driven by needs and wants. We are, by evolutionary design, selfish creatures. Human beings are wired to do what's necessary to survive, and that means we seek to fulfill our needs by any means necessary. Sometimes that means we must take advantage of other people to fill those needs and desires, and that often means the need to use dark psychology.

Most of the methods outlined in this book are about how to achieve those desires. But the one key to every method is being able to read the emotions and the mental state of others. Take time to observe the people around you. Analyze their behaviors. Compare those behaviors to your own. This will enable you to choose the way of life that you think will let you be the most successful. After all, all psychology, not just dark psychology, is about unlocking the secrets of the human mind and finding ways for us to be our best, most fulfilled selves.

By learning how to achieve your goals through the use of deception, manipulation, and the other techniques outlined here, you've learned how to use your mental and emotional power against that of others. Be sure to protect yourself from becoming a victim yourself by studying and learning the warning signs. The more adept you are at these techniques, the less susceptible you'll be at falling prey to them.

Best wishes for luck and success on your dark psychological journey!